I Do Declare!

Everyday Benefits for Everyday Believers

Julie Treimer

Copyright © 2005 by Julie Treimer

I Do Declare! Everyday Benefits for Everyday Believers
by Julie Treimer

Printed in the United States of America

ISBN 1-59781-655-8

All rights reserved solely by the author. The author guarantees all contents are original and do not infringe upon the legal rights of any other person or work. No part of this book may be reproduced in any form without the permission of the author. The views expressed in this book are not necessarily those of the publisher.

Unless otherwise indicated, all Scripture quotations in this book are from *THE MESSAGE*. Copyright by Eugene H. Peterson 1993, 1994, 1995, 1996, 2000, 2001, 2002. Used by permission of NavPress Publishing Group.

Other Scripture references are from the following sources: Scripture quotations marked (TLB) are taken from *The Living Bible*, copyright 1971. Used by permission of Tyndale House Publishers, Inc., Wheaton, Illinois 60189. All rights reserved. Scripture quotations marked (NLT) are taken from the *Holy Bible, New Living Translation*, copyright 1996. Used by permission of Tyndale House Publishers, Inc., Wheaton, Illinois 60189. All rights reserved. Scripture quotations marked (NIV) are taken from the *Holy Bible, New International Version*®. NIV®. Copyright 1973, 1978, 1984 by International Bible Society. Used by permission of Zondervan. All rights reserved. Scripture quotations marked (RSV) are taken from the *Revised Standard Version of the Bible*, copyright 1952 [2nd edition, 1971] by the Division of Christian Education of the National Council of the Churches of Christ in the United States of America. Used by permission. All rights reserved.

Unless otherwise indicated, all Scriptures in the Declarations are the author's paraphrase.

www.xulonpress.com

To my God
who is the love of my life.

To my husband, Trent
whose companionship I cherish.

To my children, Alli, Joshua, Nathaniel, and Anna
for their unending patience during this project.

To my mother, Loretta Anderson
who has always believed in me and been there for me.

To my friend, Dana Bromley
whose God-given abilities and dedication made this vision a reality.

CONTENTS

Introduction 15
The Benefit of Abundant Life 17
    A Better Life Than You Ever Dreamed Possible! 17
    The Good Shepherd 18
    My Own Sheep Know Me 19
The Benefit of Being Set Apart 20
    You Have a New Identity 20
    God's Holy People 21
    A Life Blazing with Holiness 22
The Benefit of Community 23
    The Ideal Community 23
    The Enormous Eye Monster 24
    Every Part Dependent on Every Other Part 25
The Benefit of Contentment 26
    Praise from a Maximum Security Cell 26
    Many Difficult Conditions 27
    The Recipe for Contentment 28
The Benefit of Courage 29
    The Courage to Stand Alone 29
    No Jesus, Know Fear—Know Jesus, No Fear 30
    The Baal Prophets See That Jehovah Is God! 31
The Benefit of Faith 32
    Jesus: The Object of a Roman Captain's Faith 32
    The Army Captain Understood Authority 33
    Jesus Makes a Public Example of the Captain's Faith 34
The Benefit of Freedom 35
    The Freedom of God 35
    We Choose Our Master 36
    A Dead End 37

The Benefit of a Future with Purpose 38
   Ruth's Purpose Statement 38
   The Next Step 39
   God Has Big Plans 40

The Benefit of God-Given Abilities 41
   The Master's Investment 41
   Well Done! 42
   A Terrible Way to Live 43

The Benefit of God's Comfort 44
   A Troubled World 44
   Wandering Aimlessly 45
   God Heard the Boy's Cries 46

The Benefit of God's Correction 47
   Balaam Doesn't Get His Way 47
   Falling Face Down 48
   Submitting to Discipline 49

The Benefit of God's Defense 50
   An Opportunity for Revenge 50
   Proven Innocence 51
   The Best Defense 52

The Benefit of God's Favor 53
   Hegai Is Pleased with Esther 53
   Esther Wins the Favor of Everyone 54
   If It Pleases the King 55

The Benefit of God's Forgiveness 56
   A "Certain" Man 56
   You Are That Man! 57
   The Lord Has Forgiven You 58

The Benefit of God's Goodness 59
   Jesus Is God's Goodness to You 59
   Whatever God Wants 60
   Mary's Response 61

The Benefit of God's Guidance 62

Put On Your Traveling Clothes	62
No Shortcuts!	63
Forward, March!'	64
The Benefit of God's Help	**65**
First Call for Help	65
He Still Lands in the Lion's Den!	66
God Sent His Angel	67
The Benefit of God's Love	**68**
The Son Went His Own Way	68
I Don't Deserve to Be Called Your Son	69
A Welcome Home Party	70
The Benefit of God's Mercy	**71**
God Is Slow to Get Angry	71
The People of Nineveh Repented	72
God Longs to Show Mercy	73
The Benefit of God's Peace	**74**
The Beginning of Peace	74
Don't You Care If We Perish	75
Peace! Be Still!	76
The Benefit of God's Presence	**77**
They Lost Their Best Friend	77
Another Friend!	78
The Holy Spirit	79
The Benefit of God's Protection	**80**
What You Whisper in Your Bedroom	80
We're Surrounded!	81
Your Armor	82
The Benefit of God's Provision	**83**
Your Provider	83
Last Meal	84
A Supply That Won't Run Dry	85
The Benefit of God's Righteousness	**86**
You Are Declared Righteous	86

    You Can't Earn God's Acceptance 87
    Ceremonies Don't Make You Right 88
The Benefit of God's Strength 89
    Your Own Strength 89
    The Runt of the Litter 90
    God's Might! 91
The Benefit of God's Word 92
    A Good Weed N' Feed Program 92
    God's Word Is Alive and Active 93
    Jesus Obeyed God's Word 94
The Benefit of Good Judgment 95
    Abigail Takes Action 95
    The Heart of the Matter 96
    Many Are Blessed Because of Good Judgment 97
The Benefit of Healing 98
    She Heard About Jesus 98
    The Moment She Touched Him She Was Healed 99
    Live Well, Live Blessed! 100
The Benefit of Hope 101
    She Had No Children 101
    Give Me a Son 102
    Baby Samuel 103
The Benefit of Humility 104
    A Towel Around His Waist 104
    Wash My Feet? 105
    I Have Given You an Example to Follow 106
The Benefit of Inheritance 107
    You Are an Heir 107
    No More Evil 108
    I Am Making All Things New! 109
The Benefit of Joy 110
    Jesus Called Him by Name 110
    Great Excitement and Joy 111

The Joy of His Salvation	112

The Benefit of a New Heart 113
    Paul Tried to Destroy the Church 113
    Paul Had a Change of Heart 114
    A New Life Begins 115

The Benefit of Perseverance 116
    The Long Shipbuilding Project 116
    The Long Ride 117
    The Destination 118

The Benefit of Personal Growth 119
    Nursing Babes 119
    God Makes You Grow 120
    Gardening Tools 121

The Benefit of Praise 122
    Jehoshaphat's Prayer 122
    Praise Songs 123
    Garments of Praise 124

The Benefit of Prayer 125
    The Church Prayed 125
    Rhoda Forgot to Open the Door 126
    They Didn't Recognize the Answer 127

The Benefit of Prosperity 128
    Jehovah's Blessings 128
    Streaked and Spotted Lambs and Kids 129
    God Made Me Wealthy 130

The Benefit of Reconciliation 131
    Payback Time 131
    Forgive Us 132
    Am I God? 133

The Benefit of Resisting Temptation 134
    Joseph Has Great Success 134
    A Great Sin Against God 135
    No Temptation Is Irresistible 136

- The Benefit of Rest 137
  - God Rested 137
  - Jesus Rested 138
  - Mary Rested 139
- The Benefit of Restoration 140
  - A Hand Restored 140
  - A Life Restored 141
  - A Home Restored 142
- The Benefit of Satisfaction 143
  - Living Water...143
  - Satisfaction Guaranteed 144
  - Give Me This Water 145
- The Benefit of Security 146
  - A Cork in the Storm 146
  - We're Going to Make It 147
  - Security in a Lifeboat? 148
- The Benefit of Self-Control 149
  - Food and Wine from the King's Table 149
  - Daniel's Resolve...150
  - No Equal..151
- The Benefit of Success 152
  - The Lord Will Make Your Mission Successful 152
  - The Servant Asked for a Sign 153
  - The Right Path...154
- The Benefit of Thanksgiving 155
  - An Attitude of Gratitude 155
  - Give Thanks to the Lord...156
  - In Everything Give Thanks 157
- The Benefit of Trust...158
  - A Little Boat—A Lot of Trust...158
  - Don't Put Your Confidence in People 159
  - To Know God Is to Trust God 160
- The Benefit of Victory in Battle 161

- The Right Mindset for Battle 161
- The Battle Belongs to the Lord 162
- Victory Over My Enemy 163

The Benefit of Waiting on God 164
- God's Timing Is Impeccable 164
- If Only You Had Been Here 165
- So That They Might Believe 166

The Benefit of Wisdom 167
- No Wisdom Apart from God 167
- Everyday Wisdom 168
- The Wisdom Test 169

The Benefit of Worth 170
- In His Image 170
- He Thought You Were Worth Dying For 171
- I Have Called You Friends 172

INTRODUCTION

This book is about my favorite subject—God. I grow to know Him and love Him and see His goodness more every day. I believe this book will help you do the same.

God makes so many benefits available to us as believers. For various reasons, however, we often lose sight of all He has for us. Life distracts us, or we think His blessings are for other Christians, or we fail to spend enough time getting to know Him through His Word.

God wants to be a relevant, penetrating Presence in our everyday lives, rather than some disconnected Sunday accomplishment. And because we still live in the real world and still experience everyday struggles, we need an everyday God who makes a real difference. God equips us with everything we need to live victoriously in all things. It is my hope that this book enables you to remember and make use of the tremendous benefits available to you, just when you need them.

Within each benefit, you'll find a Scripture passage that illustrates God's activity in the lives of His people. And you'll discover how He wants to participate in our lives today. You will also find powerful Scriptural declarations. Use these declarations to speak God's Word emphatically and authoritatively into your life. In doing so, you give God a direct invitation to reign in your life and circumstance. Then your feelings won't rule, evil can't reign, and other people's opinions won't matter.

I Do Declare contains fifty-two God-given benefits. Meditate on one benefit per week over the course of a year, or, during a particular struggle, meditate on the appropriate benefit. Each benefit includes a set of challenging questions and an action point that can be used personally or in the context of a small group. I almost guarantee that your relationship with God will grow more intimate and vital, and that your life will be supercharged through these benefits.

I anticipate you'll be refreshed, reloaded, and renewed as you consider God's heart toward you. And, your enthusiasm to have the living God active in your life will be contagiously evident!

> *That is what is meant by the Scriptures which say that no mere man has ever seen, heard, or even imagined what wonderful things God has ready for those who love the Lord.*
> —1 Corinthians 2:9–10 TLB

The Benefit of Abundant Life—I
A Better Life Than You Ever Dreamed Possible!

"I am the Gate for the sheep. All those others are up to no good—sheep stealers, every one of them. But the sheep didn't listen to them. I am the Gate. Anyone who goes through me will be cared for—will freely go in and out, and find pasture. A thief is only there to steal and kill and destroy. I came so they can have real and eternal life, more and better life than they ever dreamed of."
—John 10:7–10

Jesus is the only gateway to true life. We'll find true life nowhere else, not in any other pasture. In His pasture, we never lack and it is always green on His side of the fence. Also, our life-cup overflows. In today's terms, Jesus gives extreme life—we couldn't squeeze any more out of it.

We are wonderfully cared for by the One who knows us the most and loves us the best. We have security knowing that nothing and no one can remove us from His care. And we have complete protection from the evil one, who tries to steal, kill, and destroy everything God-given in our lives.

The "Abundant Life" Challenge

- Are you experiencing the extreme life that God designed for you to live?
- What might be preventing you from squeezing the most out of life?
- Reflect on the ways Jesus gives you true life.

The "Abundant Life" Declarations

Father, you have made known to me the path of life; you will fill me with joy in your presence, with eternal pleasures at your right hand.
Psalm 16:11

You came that I might have life, and might have it abundantly.
John 10:10

The Benefit of Abundant Life—II
The Good Shepherd

"I am the Good Shepherd. The Good Shepherd puts the sheep before himself, sacrifices himself if necessary. A hired man is not a real shepherd. The sheep mean nothing to him. He sees a wolf come and runs for it, leaving the sheep to be ravaged and scattered by the wolf. He's only in it for the money. The sheep don't matter to him."
—John 10:11–13

Jesus, the Good Shepherd, puts us before Himself. He demonstrated this when He died on the cross for us. Jesus was the perfect sacrifice for our sins. He tore down the curtain that separated us from God and opened up a spiritual lifeline.

Jesus is also our permanent priest who continues to intercede for us so we can have the very best life—not a second-rate one.

The "Abundant Life" Challenge

- Are you settling for a second-rate life?
- How do you feel knowing that Jesus is your "Good Shepherd?"
- List the ways Jesus has proven that His sheep matter to Him.

The "Abundant Life" Declarations

Father, you have set before me life or death, blessings or curses. I choose life and blessings! I choose to love and to obey you. I will cling to you, for you are my life and the length of my days.
Deuteronomy 30:19–20

You are the fountain of life.
Psalm 36:9

The Benefit of Abundant Life—III
My Own Sheep Know Me

"I am the Good Shepherd. I know my own sheep and my own sheep know me. In the same way, the Father knows me and I know the Father. I put the sheep before myself, sacrificing myself if necessary. You need to know that I have other sheep in addition to those in this pen. I need to gather and bring them, too. They'll also recognize my voice. Then it will be one flock, one Shepherd."
—John 10:14–16

The key to true life is a life-giving relationship with the Good Shepherd. When you know Him, you desperately desire to know Him more.

Spend time every day nurturing this relationship as the most important one in your life. As you do, you'll experience maximum joy, love, hope, and peace. You'll recognize His voice as He speaks to you about your life. You'll gain a life filled with purpose and meaning. You will enthusiastically face the gift of a new day and its many possibilities. And all your other relationships will have a new richness and depth.

The "Abundant Life" Challenge

- Do you recognize His voice in your life?
- How does your relationship with God enhance your other relationships?
- Spend time telling God you desire to know Him more.

The "Abundant Life" Declarations

Father, this is real and eternal life: knowing you, the one and only true God, and Jesus Christ, whom you sent.
John 17:3

If I cling to my life, I will lose it; but if I give it up for you, I will save it.
Matthew 10:39

The Benefit of Being Set Apart—I
You Have a New Identity

Never again shall you be called "The God-forsaken Land" or the "Land That God Forgot." Your new name will be "The Land of God's Delight" and "The Bride," for the Lord delights in you and will claim you as his own.
—Isaiah 62:4 TLB

God called you to be His own. You can now find your identity in Him. You are an heir to all His promises. He delights in you.

God called you out of the darkness into His marvelous light, uniquely qualifying you to reflect Him to this world and to bring Him glory. God called and equipped you to tell others about His love. You have been chosen.

The "Being Set Apart" Challenge

- Do you see yourself as God's treasured possession, His delight?
- What would living in your new identity look like in everyday life?
- Ask God to allow you to be His reflection to someone today.

The "Being Set Apart" Declarations

Father, I am part of a chosen generation, a royal priesthood, a holy nation, your own special people, that I may proclaim your praises; you called me out of darkness into your marvelous light. We once were not a people but are now the people of God, who had not obtained mercy but now have obtained mercy.
1 Peter 2:9–10

We are a people holy to you. Out of all the peoples on the face of the earth, you have chosen us to be your treasured possession.
Deuteronomy 14:2

The Benefit of Being Set Apart—II
God's Holy People

See, the Lord has sent his messengers to every land and said, "Tell my people, I, the Lord your God, am coming to save you and will bring you many gifts." And they shall be called "The Holy People" and "The Lord's Redeemed," and Jerusalem shall be called "The Land of Desire" and "The City God Has Blessed."
—Isaiah 62:11–12 TLB

The word *holy* signifies being "separated or set apart for God." By this definition, you became holy the moment you believed in Jesus as your Savior.

From the beginning, God has desired people who were holy. He wants people to worship Him alone, to be wholeheartedly devoted to Him. He is not interested in sharing your affections with any other "gods." He wants your time and attention. He wants you to love Him with all your heart, soul, mind, and strength. He wants you to serve Him alone. And He wants your best, not your leftovers.

The "Being Set Apart" Challenge

- Are you wholeheartedly devoted to God, or are you divided in your affections?
- Do you give Him your best, or your leftovers?
- In all you do today, commit to give God your best.

The "Being Set Apart" Declarations

Father, there was a time when I was a sinner, but now my sins are washed away, and I am set apart for you; and you have accepted me because of what the Lord Jesus Christ and your Spirit have done for me.
1 Corinthians 6:11

I know that you are God and you made me. I am yours—a well cared for sheep in your pasture.
Psalm 100:3

The Benefit of Being Set Apart—III
A Life Blazing with Holiness

Don't lazily slip back into those old grooves of evil, doing just what you feel like doing. You didn't know any better then; you do now. As obedient children, let yourselves be pulled into a way of life shaped by God's life, a life energetic and blazing with holiness.
—1 Peter 1:13–15

Only Jesus has achieved perfect holiness of character and behavior. But, you are being transformed into His likeness more every day. It is vitally important to make His holy character and behavior your life's goal.

You are a living letter read by everyone. You must be distinct from your culture, distinct in your beliefs and how you live them. If you blend in with your culture, you will lose your saltiness. You need to reveal God to others by being salt and light. They will take notice of the difference and be able to taste and see God through you.

The "Being Set Apart" Challenge

- Do you blend in with the culture around you, or are you set apart from it?
- Which is vitally important to you, holiness or doing whatever you want to do?
- List three ways you've been transformed by God.

The "Being Set Apart" Declarations

Father, your Son gave himself for us to redeem us from all wickedness and to purify for himself a people that are his very own, eager to do what is good.
Titus 2:14

I desire to be holy now in everything I do, just as you are holy, who invited me to be your child. You have said "I must be holy, for you are holy."
1 Peter 1:15–16

The Benefit of Community—I
The Ideal Community

I want you to think about how all this makes you more significant, not less. A body isn't just a single part blown up into something huge. It's all the different-but-similar parts arranged and functioning together.

If Foot said, "I'm not elegant like Hand, embellished with rings; I guess I don't belong to this body," would that make it so? If Ear said, "I'm not beautiful like Eye, limpid and expressive; I don't deserve a place on the head," would you want to remove it from the body?

If the body was all eye, how could it hear? If all ear, how could it smell? As it is, we see that God has carefully placed each part of the body right where he wanted it.
—1 Corinthians 12:12–20

By God's design, Christians never have to go through life alone. God intends for us to be part of a community of believers, having a place where we belong and fit in. In this community, we should devote ourselves to one another in brotherly love. And we fellowship together on the deepest level because we have the same Spirit.

The "Community" Challenge

- Are you trying to live your Christian life apart from the Body of Christ?
- Do you believe you are a significant part of God's community of believers?
- Identify ways you can add value to your community of believers.

The "Community" Declarations

Father, as I live in the light of your presence, just as Christ does, then I will have wonderful fellowship and joy with others.
1 John 1:7

I will consider how I may spur others on toward love and good deeds. I will not give up meeting with other Christians.
Hebrews 10:24–25

The Benefit of Community—II
The Enormous Eye Monster

But I also want you to think about how this keeps your significance from getting blown up into self-importance. For no matter how significant you are, it is only because of what you are a part of. An enormous eye or a gigantic hand wouldn't be a body, but a monster. What we have is one body with many parts, each its proper size and in its proper place. No part is important on its own. Can you imagine Eye telling Hand, "Get lost; I don't need you?" Or, Head telling Foot, "You're fired; your job has been phased out?"

As a matter of fact, in practice it works the other way—the "lower" the part, the more basic, and therefore necessary. You can live without an eye, for instance, but not without a stomach. When it's a part of your own body you are concerned with, it makes no difference whether the part is visible or clothed, higher or lower.
—1 Corinthians 12:21–24

Some parts just can't seem to fit in, some are ignored, some get all the glory, some think they're more important than others, many can't stop comparing their part to all the other parts. Here's where grace, forgiveness, mercy, and prayer go a long way.

The "Community" Challenge

- In your community of believers, do you expect high visibility?
- Do you make allowances for other's shortcomings, or do you gossip about them?
- Send a card to encourage someone today.

The "Community" Declarations

Father, I will be kind to others, tenderhearted, forgiving them, just as you have forgiven me because I belong to Christ.
Ephesians 4:32

I will encourage others and build them up.
1 Thessalonians 5:11

The Benefit of Community—III
Every Part Dependent on Every Other Part

The way God designed our bodies is a model for understanding our lives together as a church: every part dependent on every other part, the parts we mention and the parts we don't, the parts we see and the parts we don't. If one part hurts, every other part is involved in the hurt, and in the healing. If one part flourishes, every other part enters into the exuberance.

You are Christ's body—that's who you are! You must never forget this. Only as you accept your part of that body does your "part" mean anything.
—1 Corinthians 12:26–27

Christians need to practice the "one anothers" found in Scripture. We need to accept one another as Christ accepted us, honor one another, bear one another's burdens, teach one another, hold one another accountable, encourage one another, and pray for one another.

Remember, your part in this community is vital. And life is just so much sweeter when we do it together.

The "Community" Challenge

▸ Are you practicing the "one anothers" in God's community of believers?
▸ How have you benefited by doing life together with others?
▶▶ Join a small group of believers where you can grow and contribute.

The "Community" Declarations

Father, I will be humble, gentle and patient with others, making allowance for their faults because of your love. I will try always to be led along together with others in the body by the Holy Spirit and so be at peace with others.
Ephesians 4:2–3

When your children are in need, I want to be the one to help them out.
Romans 12:13

The Benefit of Contentment—I
Praise from a Maximum Security Cell

The judges went along with the mob, had Paul and Silas's clothes ripped off and ordered a public beating. After beating them black-and-blue, they threw them into jail, telling the jailkeeper to put them under heavy guard so there would be no chance of escape. He did just that—threw them into the maximum security cell in the jail and clamped leg irons on them.

Along about midnight, Paul and Silas were at prayer and singing a robust hymn to God.

—Acts 16:22–25

Perfect circumstances do not equate to contentment. The life of Paul makes this very clear. He was a well-educated Jew and a highly respected Pharisee with a lot of authority. He zealously obeyed God's laws. Paul was definitely on the fast track to success.

Then Jesus Christ came into his life and changed him. Was Paul content before he became a follower of Christ? There's no indication that he was. Yet in this Scripture he sits in leg irons, praising God! Contentment is not circumstance based.

The "Contentment" Challenge

- Is your contentment based on how comfortable your life is?
- Do you think you would be content if only…?
- Memorize Hebrews 13:5.

The "Contentment" Declarations

Father, my contentment is not in wealth but in seeing you, and knowing all is well between us.

Psalm 17:15

I can be content with what I have, because you have said, you will never leave me nor forsake me.

Hebrews 13:5

The Benefit of Contentment—II
Many Difficult Conditions

I've been shipwrecked three times, and immersed in the open sea for a night and a day. In hard traveling year in and year out, I've had to ford rivers, fend off robbers, struggle with friends, struggle with foes. I've been at risk in the city, at risk in the country, endangered by desert sun and sea storm, and betrayed by those I thought were my brothers. I've known drudgery and hard labor, many a long and lonely night without sleep, many a missed meal, blasted by the cold, naked to the weather.
—2 Corinthians 11:25–27

Paul's number one priority was not to have an easy, comfortable life, but to live for Christ. Perhaps we need to change our priorities. Paul focused on eternal things more than on temporal things. Maybe we should change our focus. Paul continually remembered all that he had in Christ, and he was incredibly grateful. We might need to change our attitudes.

We can learn to be more like Paul or we can end up like Eve. Eve had paradise at her fingertips. She was content until Satan deceived her into desiring the one thing she didn't and couldn't have. I'm sure that both Paul and Eve would testify to the truth that contentment is great gain.

The "Contentment" Challenge

- In terms of "stuff," when is enough, enough?
- Why do you think contentment is great gain?
- Evaluate your priorities for today, and make them eternity focused.

The "Contentment" Declarations

Father, I know that Godliness with contentment is great gain. For I brought nothing into the world, and I can take nothing out of it.
1 Timothy 6:6–8

Because you are my Shepherd, I have everything I need!
Psalm 23:1

The Benefit of Contentment—III
The Recipe for Contentment

I've learned by now to be quite content whatever my circumstances. I'm just as happy with little as with much, with much as with little. I've found the recipe for being happy whether full or hungry, hands full or hands empty. Whatever I have, wherever I am, I can make it through anything in the One who makes me who I am.
—Philippians 4:11–13

It's amazing to me that Paul could say "I've learned by now to be quite content whatever my circumstances." But it's also quite comforting to me that Paul had to learn contentment. Becoming a Christian didn't make Paul instantly content in all circumstances. That means there's hope for you and me!

Discontentment can eat you up, if you continue down that road. We really do have everything when we have Christ. Let's stop chasing after temporary highs. Let's be happy for people when God blesses them in a big way. Let's complement our Maker and tell Him we're happy for the way He made us. And let's spend more time pursuing Christ, Who said He would never leave us. I know we'll all enjoy life a lot more. This truly is the good life, right now—not after we win the lottery.

The "Contentment" Challenge

- How do you respond when God greatly blesses someone else?
- Do you believe you can make it through anything with Christ?
- Meditate on Paul's recipe for contentment.

The "Contentment" Declarations

Father, I have everything because I have you.
Colossians 2:10

Your grace is sufficient for me.
2 Corinthians 12:9

The Benefit of Courage—I
The Courage to Stand Alone

Then Elijah spoke again. "I am the only prophet of the Lord who is left," he told them, "but Baal has 450 prophets. Now bring two young bulls. The prophets of Baal may choose whichever one they wish and cut it into pieces and lay it on the wood of their altar, but without putting any fire under the wood; and I will prepare the other young bull and lay it on the wood on the Lord's altar, with no fire under it.

Then pray to your god, and I will pray to the Lord; and the god who answers by sending fire to light the wood is the true God!" And all the people agreed to this test.
—1 Kings 18:22–24 TLB

Every time God asked someone in Scripture to take a risk, to seize a divine opportunity rather than playing it safe, incredible things happened. The 450 prophets of Baal did not intimidate Elijah, even though he was greatly outnumbered.

He let his confidence in God, not his fear, rule his actions. His boldness came from knowing who God was.

The "Courage" Challenge

- Are you more interested in pleasing God, or in pleasing man?
- Do you play it safe, refusing to seize a divine opportunity, because you don't want to fail?
- Let your confidence in God rule your actions today.

The "Courage" Declarations

Father, you will never fail me nor forsake me. Therefore I will not doubt or fear. You are my Helper, and I am not afraid of anything that mere man can do to me.
Hebrews 13:5–6

I will not fear death, for you are close beside me, guarding and guiding me all the way.
Psalm 23:4

The Benefit of Courage—II
No Jesus, Know Fear—Know Jesus, No Fear

Then Elijah turned to the prophets of Baal. "You first," he said, "for there are many of you; choose one of the bulls and prepare it and call to your god; but don't put any fire under the wood."

So they prepared one of the young bulls and placed it on the altar; and they called to Baal all morning, shouting, "O Baal, hear us!" But there was no reply of any kind. Then they began to dance around the altar. About noontime, Elijah began mocking them.

"You'll have to shout louder than that," he scoffed, "to catch the attention of your god! Perhaps he is talking to someone, or is out sitting on the toilet, or maybe he is away on a trip, or is asleep and needs to be wakened!"

So they shouted louder and, as was their custom, cut themselves with knives and swords until the blood gushed out. They raved all afternoon until the time of the evening sacrifice, but there was no reply, no voice, no answer.

—1 Kings 18:25–29 TLB

Elijah felt no fear because he knew that Baal held no power over him. Don't empower your fears—empower your faith. Fear imprisons us, *but Jesus* gives us a "Get-Out-of-Jail-Free" card!

The "Courage" Challenge

- What is your greatest fear?
- If God is for you, who can stand against you?
- Use your Get-Out-of-Jail-Free card to be released from your greatest fear.

The "Courage" Declarations

Father, you are my light and my salvation and the stronghold of my life—of whom shall I be afraid?

Psalm 27:1

I did not receive a spirit of bondage again to fear, but I received the Spirit of adoption.

Romans 8:15

The Benefit of Courage—III
The Baal Prophets See That Jehovah Is God!

At the customary time for offering the evening sacrifice, Elijah walked up to the altar and prayed, "O Lord, God of Abraham, Isaac, and Israel, prove today that you are the God of Israel and that I am your servant; prove that I have done all this at your command.

"O Lord, answer me! Answer me so these people will know that you are God and that you have brought them back to yourself."

Then, suddenly, fire flashed down from heaven and burned up the young bull, the wood, the stones, the dust, and even evaporated all the water in the ditch!

And when the people saw it, they fell to their faces upon the ground shouting, "Jehovah is God! Jehovah is God!"
—1 Kings 18:36–39 TLB

If God asks you to get out of the safe-boat, keep your eyes on Him, not on the circumstances or the people around you. Don't let fear steal the opportunities God has given you.

The "Courage" Challenge

- Is God asking you to get out of the boat in some area of your life?
- Is God the source of fear? If not, who or what is?
- Courageously show to someone today that Jehovah is God.

The "Courage" Declarations

Father, you did not give me a spirit of timidity, but a spirit of power, of love and of self-discipline.
2 Timothy 1:7

I will be of good courage, and you will strengthen my heart, because my hope is in you.
Psalm 31:24

The Benefit of Faith—I
Jesus: The Object of a Roman Captain's Faith

When [Jesus] finished speaking to the people, he entered Capernaum. A Roman captain there had a servant who was on his deathbed. He prized him highly and didn't want to lose him.

When he heard Jesus was back, he sent leaders from the Jewish community asking him to come and heal his servant. They came to Jesus and urged him to do it, saying, "He deserves this. He loves our people. He even built our meeting place."

—Luke 7:1–6

Faith is the confident assurance that what we hope for is going to happen—even before we see any signs of it.

In this story, the Roman captain wanted his servant healed because the servant was very important to him. Notice that the captain didn't send for just anyone to heal his servant, he sent for Jesus.

Faith is not wishing really hard for what you want. Faith is connecting your God-given desires with the One who will make it happen.

The "Faith" Challenge

▸ What is the difference between wishing for something and putting your faith in Jesus?
▸ How can you know if your desires are God-given?
▶▶ Remember a specific time when you walked by faith and not by sight.

The "Faith" Declarations

Father, I believe that you exist and that you reward those who earnestly seek you.

Hebrews 11:6

By faith I am sure of what I hope for and certain of what I do not see.

Hebrews 11:1

The Benefit of Faith—II
The Army Captain Understood Authority

Jesus went with them. When he was still quite far from the house, the captain sent friends to tell him, "Master, you don't have to go to all this trouble. I'm not that good a person, you know. I'd be embarrassed for you to come to my house, even embarrassed to come to you in person. Just give the order and my servant will get well. I'm a man under orders; I also give orders. I tell one soldier, 'Go,' and he goes; another, 'Come,' and he comes; my slave, 'Do this,' and he does it."
—Luke 7:6–8

A person with authority has the power to make something happen.

Because of his position, this army captain had a great understanding of authority. In fact, he understood it so well, he didn't think Jesus needed to go to his servant. The captain knew that Jesus only needed to say the word and his servant would be healed.

The captain also understood that Jesus healing his servant didn't depend on whether or not he was a good person. He knew that Jesus, Himself, was good and that He had the power to heal.

The "Faith" Challenge

▸ Do you believe that Jesus has authority over all things?
▸ Do you approach God with humility, knowing that all power comes from Him?
▸▸ Meditate on the power available to you in Jesus' Name.

The "Faith" Declarations

Father, I am firmly persuaded that you have the power to do what you have promised.
Romans 4:21–22

You call into being that which does not exist.
Romans 4:17

The Benefit of Faith—III
Jesus Makes a Public Example of the Captain's Faith

Taken aback, Jesus addressed the accompanying crowd: "I've yet to come across this kind of simple trust anywhere in Israel, the very people who are supposed to know about God and how he works." When the messengers got back home, they found the servant up and well.
—Luke 7:9–10

Jesus was absolutely amazed by the captain's faith. So much so, He made a public example of the captain's faith. Jesus had never seen such great faith, even among those who supposedly knew God and were familiar with His ways.

Jesus gets excited when His people understand how He works, and simply believe that He will do what He says. In fact, He says that without faith, it is impossible to please Him. The captain's reward for his faith was the healing of his servant. Jesus rewards great faith.

The "Faith" Challenge

- Can Jesus point to you as an example of someone who has great faith?
- Do you take God at His word, or do you question Him?
- Study Luke 18:35–43 as another example of great faith.

The "Faith" Declarations

Father, my faith comes by hearing your Word.
Romans 10:17

I will live by faith.
Romans 1:17

The Benefit of Freedom—I
The Freedom of God

Throw yourselves wholeheartedly and full-time—remember, you've been raised from the dead!—into God's way of doing things. Sin can't tell you how to live. After all, you're not living under that old tyranny any longer. You're living in the freedom of God.
—Romans 6:13–14

God intends His people to be free from anything that enslaves them. But we sometimes have a hard time walking in God's ways, which lead us to freedom.

For example, living as slaves in Egypt, the Israelites were subject to cruel slave masters. But God miraculously delivered them from this bondage. On the victory side of the Red Sea, they sang praise songs to God.

God, then, told the Israelites to listen to Him carefully and to do what was right in His eyes. But after just a few problems and trials, they started grumbling, wishing they were back in Egypt. After all, they said, at least we had water and food in Egypt!

Sounds ridiculous, right? But sometimes we, too, choose to go back to Egypt—back to old, familiar, and destructive ways. God brought you out of bondage and into the Promised Land. Continue to choose God's freedom over the tyranny and bondage of sin.

The "Freedom" Challenge

- Are you careful to do what is right in God's eyes?
- When you face trials, to what or to whom do you turn?
- Identify your "Egypt," then turn to God for freedom.

The "Freedom" Declarations

Father, it was for freedom Christ set me free; therefore I will stand fast, and will not submit again to a yoke of slavery.
Galatians 5:1

The law of the Spirit of life in Christ Jesus made me free from the law of sin and of death.
Romans 8:2

The Benefit of Freedom—II
We Choose Our Master

Don't you realize that you can choose your own master? You can choose sin (with death) or else obedience (with acquittal). The one to whom you offer yourself—he will take you and be your master and you will be his slave.
Thank God that though you once chose to be slaves of sin, now you have obeyed with all your heart the teaching to which God has committed you. And now you are free from your old master, sin; and you have become slaves to your new master, righteousness.
—Romans 6:16–18 TLB

When Moses led the Israelites out of slavery in Egypt, life was good: they left with some Egyptian wealth, God was watching over them and guiding them, and they were no longer subjected to bitter slave labor. Yes, life was good.

But then the Egyptian army trapped them on the edge of the Red Sea. Even though the Israelites had just watched God work mighty wonders on their behalf, they feared the approaching army.

How did the Israelites react? They whined to Moses. They demanded to know why he made them leave Egypt; they insisted that slavery in Egypt was better than dying in the desert.

How foolish! Yet, every time we choose to disobey, we declare that we are better off as slaves to sin.

The "Freedom" Challenge

- What sin still seems appealing to you?
- Why is obedience to God better than slavery to sin?
- ▸▸ Declare to God that He is your Lord and you will serve Him.

The "Freedom" Declarations

Father, I am no longer a slave to sin, but I am your child. You have set me free indeed.
John 8:34–36

Where your Spirit is, there is liberty.
2 Corinthians 3:17

The Benefit of Freedom—III
A Dead End

You can readily recall, can't you, how at one time the more you did just what you felt like doing—not caring about others, not caring about God—the worse your life became and the less freedom you had? And how much different is it now as you live in God's freedom, your lives healed and expansive in holiness?

As long as you did what you felt like doing, ignoring God, you didn't have to bother with right thinking or right living, or right anything for that matter. But do you call that a free life? What did you get out of it? Nothing you're proud of now. Where did it get you? A dead end.

—Romans 6:19–21

Many unhealthy ways of living once held us captive. God wanted to not only set us free *from* all those things, but He also wanted to set us free *to* a whole new way of life. We are now free to love, free to live right, free to hope, and free to dream. Sin no longer gets to call the shots—God does.

The "Freedom" Challenge

▸ Have you allowed God to set you free to a completely new way of life?
▸ What life benefits do you see from walking in God's freedom?
▸▸ Consider whether your lifestyle choices result in freedom or in bondage.

The "Freedom" Declarations

Father, I have been bought and paid for by Christ, so I belong to you—I can be free now from all these earthly prides and fears.
1 Corinthians 7:23

I will live as though I am free, but not to do wrong. Instead I am free to do only God's will at all times.
1 Peter 2:16

The Benefit of a Future with Purpose—I
Ruth's Purpose Statement

Orpah kissed her mother-in-law good-bye; but Ruth embraced her and held on. Naomi said, "Look, your sister-in-law is going back home to live with her own people and gods; go with her."
But Ruth said, "Don't force me to leave you; don't make me go home. Where you go, I go; and where you live, I'll live. Your people are my people, your God is my god; where you die, I'll die, and that's where I'll be buried, so help me God—not even death itself is going to come between us!"

—Ruth 1:14–17

After Naomi lost her husband and sons, she decided to move back to Bethlehem, her hometown. She released her daughters-in-law, Orpah and Ruth, from any further obligation to her.

Orpah decided to take Naomi up on her offer, so she left to start a talk show in Moab (Okay, maybe not!). But Ruth was determined to stick by Naomi.

Sometimes we think that God's wonderful plans are only for super-spiritual people. Wrong! Ruth was just an ordinary woman from Moab. God had over-the-top plans for Ruth, just as He does for you.

The "Future with Purpose" Challenge

- Do you believe God has great plans only for other people?
- Do you know God can do something extraordinary in your life?
- Develop a purpose statement for your life.

The "Future with Purpose" Declarations

Father, you who have saved me and chosen me for your holy work, not because I deserved it but because that was your plan long before the world began.

2 Timothy 1:9

You will fulfill your purposes for me; You will not abandon the work of your hands.

Psalm 138:8

The Benefit of a Future with Purpose—II
The Next Step

Boaz answered her, "I've heard all about you—heard about the way you treated your mother-in-law after the death of her husband, and how you left your father and mother and the land of your birth and have come to live among a bunch of total strangers. God reward you well for what you've done—and with a generous bonus besides from God, to whom you've come seeking protection under his wings."
—Ruth 2:11–12

Naomi and Ruth "just happened" to arrive in Bethlehem at the beginning of the barley harvest. Ruth "just happened" to glean in fields that belonged to Boaz. And Boaz "just happened" to be a close relative of Naomi. God had a wonderful plan.

God's plan wasn't laid out for Ruth when she left Moab, but she did know what her next step was to be: following Naomi.

Sometimes people think that God's plan for them begins far in the future. Not so. Your future is now. God has a great purpose for your life today. And God will use things that happen today to prepare you for what's next. Begin by doing what you know is right—today.

The "Future with Purpose" Challenge

- ▸ Are you so future minded that you miss what God is doing today?
- ▸ How might God want to use you today to prepare you for what's next?
- ▸▸ Ask God to use you for His purposes today.

The "Future with Purpose" Declarations

Father, I know the plans you have for me, plans to prosper me and not to harm me, plans to give me a hope and a future.
Jeremiah 29:11

Many are the plans in my heart, but it is your purpose that prevails.
Proverbs 19:21

The Benefit of a Future with Purpose—III
God Has Big Plans

Boaz married Ruth. She became his wife. Boaz slept with her. By God's gracious gift she conceived and had a son.

The town women said to Naomi, "Blessed be God! He didn't leave you without family to carry on your life. May this baby grow up to be famous in Israel! He'll make you young again! He'll take care of you in old age. And this daughter-in-law who has brought him into the world and loves you so much, why, she's worth more to you than seven sons!"

Naomi took the baby and held him in her arms, cuddling him, cooing over him, waiting on him hand and foot.

The neighborhood women started calling him "Naomi's baby boy!" But his real name was Obed. Obed was the father of Jesse, and Jesse the father of David.

—Ruth 4:13–17

And the rest is history! David was the ancestor of Jesus, our Redeemer. So little, ordinary Ruth from Moab ends up part of God's big, holy plan. Submit to God's holy plan for your life and watch what He does.

The "Future with Purpose" Challenge

▸ What have you learned about Ruth that you can apply to your life?
▸ Does it excite you to be part of God's grand plan?
▸▸ Surrender your plans, hopes, and dreams to God.

The "Future with Purpose" Declarations

Father, I am confident that you, who began a good work in me, will carry it on to completion until the day of Christ Jesus.
Philippians 1:6

What you have said, that will you bring about; what you have planned, that will you do.
Isaiah 46:11

The Benefit of God-Given Abilities—I
The Master's Investment

"It's also like a man going off on an extended trip. He called his servants together and delegated responsibilities. To one he gave five thousand dollars, to another two thousand, to a third one thousand, depending on their abilities. Then he left.

"Right off, the first servant went to work and doubled his master's investment. The second did the same. But the man with the single thousand dug a hole and carefully buried his master's money."
—Matthew 25:14–18

Some might think the master in this parable unreasonable. But it plainly states at the beginning that the master delegated responsibilities according to the servant's abilities. He did not have expectations of them that they could not fulfill.

As we apply this parable to real life, we can draw some conclusions. But first, I want to mention one important truth that wasn't part of this story. God is the One who gives abilities to us as He sees fit. We cannot claim credit for any of our skills or talents. They are God-given and everyone has some. He invested certain abilities in you and He expects a good return on His investment.

The "God-Given Abilities" Challenge

▸ Do you take credit for the special skills or talents you have?
▸ Are you giving God a good return on His investment?
▸▸ Take steps this week to discover your God-given abilities.

The "God-Given Abilities" Declarations

Father, you give me the ability to produce wealth.
Deuteronomy 8:18

You have given each of us the ability to do certain things well.
Romans 12:6

The Benefit of God-Given Abilities—II
Well Done!

"After a long absence, the master of those three servants came back and settled up with them. The one given five thousand dollars showed him how he had doubled his investment. His master commended him: 'Good work! You did your job well. From now on be my partner.'

"The servant with the two thousand showed how he also had doubled his master's investment. His master commended him: 'Good work! You did your job well. From now on be my partner.'

"The servant given one thousand said, 'Master, I know you have high standards and hate careless ways, that you demand the best and make no allowances for error. I was afraid I might disappoint you, so I found a good hiding place and secured your money. Here it is, safe and sound down to the last cent.'"

—Matthew 25:19–25

"Well done, good and faithful servant!" Those are undoubtedly some of the sweetest words you'll ever hear from God.

Never let fear of failing or disappointing God keep you from using the skills and abilities He has given you. God would be more disappointed if you made no effort at all.

The "God-Given Abilities" Challenge

▸ Do you feel you have failed or disappointed God in some way?
▸ How can you grow in your God-given abilities?
▸▸ Call one of God's faithful servants to say, "Well done."

The "God-Given Abilities" Declarations

Father, you have given each of us special abilities—whatever you want us to have—out of your rich storehouse of gifts.
Ephesians 4:7

I will guard well the splendid, God-given ability I received as a gift from the Holy Spirit who lives within me.
2 Timothy 1:14

The Benefit of God-Given Abilities—III
A Terrible Way to Live

"The master was furious. 'That's a terrible way to live! It's criminal to live cautiously like that! If you knew I was after the best, why did you do less than the least? The least you could have done would have been to invest the sum with the bankers, where at least I would have gotten a little interest.

"'Take the thousand and give it to the one who risked the most. And get rid of this "play-it-safe" who won't go out on a limb. Throw him out into utter darkness.'"

—Matthew 25:26–30

God seems less than impressed when we play it safe with His investments. He wants a bigger market share and He needs partners willing to make that happen.

God expects us to generously invest everything He's given us—time, money, gifts, skills, and talents—into the lives of others. He wants us to go out on a limb, because that's where the fruit is.

The servant who is faithful with what God gives him will be given even more. Take a risk with God today. Use it or lose it!

The "God-Given Abilities" Challenge

▸ Do you typically play it safe, or are you a risk taker?
▸ Are you willing to go out on a limb for God?
▸▸ Invest yourself in someone's life today.

The "God-Given Abilities" Declarations

Father, I will use my special abilities to help others, passing on to them many kinds of blessings.

1 Peter 4:10

When I use well what you have given to me, I will be given more, and shall have abundance.

Matthew 25:29

The Benefit of God's Comfort—I
A Troubled World

And Sarah declared, "God has brought me laughter! All who hear about this will laugh with me. For who would have dreamed that I would ever have a baby? Yet I have given Abraham a son in his old age!"

As time went by and Isaac grew and was weaned, Abraham gave a big party to celebrate the happy occasion. But Sarah saw Ishmael—the son of Abraham and her Egyptian servant Hagar—making fun of Isaac. So she turned to Abraham and demanded, "Get rid of that servant and her son. He is not going to share the family inheritance with my son, Isaac. I won't have it!"
—Genesis 21:6–10 NLT

In this world, you will have trouble, hardship, pain, suffering, and difficulties. Even Christians experience these things. But God's presence makes the difference.

Hagar and Ishmael got kicked out of town because Sarah was fed up with them. But God kept a close watch on everything. He was not distant, cold, or uncaring to their circumstances. On the contrary, He was very near and ready to console.

As you walk through the valley, remember that God is walking with you. He wants to hold you close and reassure you.

The "God's Comfort" Challenge

- Do you believe God watches over you?
- Do difficulties bring you closer to God?
- Invite God into your circumstance today—and He will draw near to you.

The "God's Comfort" Declarations

Father, when doubts fill my mind, when my heart is in turmoil, you quiet me and give me renewed hope and cheer.
Psalm 94:19

When I am downcast, You will comfort me.
2 Corinthians 7:6

The Benefit of God's Comfort—II
Wandering Aimlessly

This upset Abraham very much because Ishmael was his son. But God told Abraham, "Do not be upset over the boy and your servant wife. Do just as Sarah says, for Isaac is the son through whom your descendants will be counted. But I will make a nation of the descendants of Hagar's son because he also is your son."

So Abraham got up early the next morning, prepared food for the journey, and strapped a container of water to Hagar's shoulders. He sent her away with their son, and she walked out into the wilderness of Beersheba, wandering aimlessly.

When the water was gone, she left the boy in the shade of a bush. Then she went and sat down by herself about a hundred yards away. "I don't want to watch the boy die," she said, as she burst into tears.
—Genesis 21:11–16 NLT

Hagar and Ishmael were sent to wander aimlessly in the desert with little provision. Now that would be distressing!

Sometimes in the midst of our pain, we wander aimlessly and don't know where to turn. Some turn to a bottle, some to relationships, while others try entertainment. But the truth is, when you turn to God you will never be disappointed—you will find comfort.

The "God's Comfort" Challenge

- Do you wander aimlessly during painful times?
- Do you believe that God wants to ease your pain?
- Reach out today to someone who is wandering aimlessly.

The "God's Comfort" Declarations

You are the Father of compassion and the God of all comfort. You comfort me in all my troubles, so that I can comfort those in any trouble.
2 Corinthians 1:3–4

Your Word is a comfort to me.
Psalm 119:52

The Benefit of God's Comfort—III
God Heard the Boy's Cries

Then God heard the boy's cries, and the angel of God called to Hagar from the sky, "Hagar, what's wrong? Do not be afraid! God has heard the boy's cries from the place where you laid him. Go to him and comfort him, for I will make a great nation from his descendants."

Then God opened Hagar's eyes, and she saw a well. She immediately filled her water container and gave the boy a drink. And God was with the boy as he grew up in the wilderness of Paran.
—Genesis 21:17–20 NLT

Aren't you glad God hears our cries? He not only heard Ishmael's cries, but He also sent encouragement. God wanted to calm Hagar and Ishmael's fears and give them hope for the future.

In our trying times, it's difficult to see or think clearly. We're blinded by doubts, fears, and a sense of hopelessness. But God wants to step into our situation, dry our tears, calm our fears, and offer hope.

God opened Hagar's eyes, and He wants to open ours to see how He works in the midst of troubling circumstances. God is an oasis of comfort and hope in the wilderness.

The "God's Comfort" Challenge

- Are you in a situation that you feel is hopeless?
- Do you know God hears your cries?
- Consider ways God might be working in your difficult situation.

The "God's Comfort" Declarations

Father, you gave me a Comforter, who is the Holy Spirit, so that you may abide with me forever.
John 14:16

As a mother comforts her child, so you will comfort me.
Isaiah 66:13

The Benefit of God's Correction—I
Balaam Doesn't Get His Way

So the next morning Balaam saddled his donkey and started off with the Moabite officials. But God was furious that Balaam was going, so he sent the angel of the Lord to stand in the road to block his way.

As Balaam and two servants were riding along, Balaam's donkey suddenly saw the angel of the Lord standing in the road with a drawn sword in his hand. The donkey bolted off the road into a field, but Balaam beat it and turned it back onto the road.

Then the angel of the Lord stood at a place where the road narrowed between two vineyard walls. When the donkey saw the angel of the Lord standing there, it tried to squeeze by and crushed Balaam's foot against the wall. So Balaam beat the donkey again.

Then the angel of the Lord moved farther down the road and stood in a place so narrow that the donkey could not get by at all. This time when the donkey saw the angel, it lay down under Balaam. In a fit of rage Balaam beat it again with his staff.
—Numbers 22:21–27 NLT

God loves us too much to let us continue in our folly. Let Him lovingly redirect you. Father knows best!

The "God's Correction" Challenge

- Do you stubbornly do things your own way?
- Do you get discouraged when God corrects you?
- Think about a time when God's discipline brought you life and health.

The "God's Correction" Declarations

Father, I won't be angry when you discipline me. I won't be discouraged when you have to show me where I am wrong.
Hebrews 12:5–6

Your discipline is good and leads to life and health.
Isaiah 38:16

The Benefit of God's Correction—II
Falling Face Down

Then the Lord caused the donkey to speak. "What have I done to you that deserves your beating me these three times?" it asked Balaam.
"Because you have made me look like a fool!" Balaam shouted. "If I had a sword with me, I would kill you!"
"But I am the same donkey you always ride on," the donkey answered. "Have I ever done anything like this before?"
"No," he admitted.
Then the Lord opened Balaam's eyes, and he saw the angel of the Lord standing in the roadway with a drawn sword in his hand. Balaam fell face down on the ground before him.
—Numbers 22:28–31 NLT

Some people, like Balaam, have to learn things the hard way. Parents understand this well when they watch their children rebel against instruction. Children do not like to be told what to do. They want to do things their own way and they don't easily admit when they're wrong.

Some of us have not matured beyond that childlike behavior. God didn't give up on Balaam, no matter how stubborn he was. And God will not give up on you either.

The "God's Correction" Challenge
- Do you have to learn things the hard way?
- Do you ask God to help you learn from His correction?
- ▸▸ Ask God to help you turn from any rebellion in your heart.

The "God's Correction" Declarations
Father, I will not resent it when you chasten and correct me, for your punishment is proof of your love. Just as a father punishes a son he delights in to make him better, so you correct me.
Proverbs 3:11

After you have corrected me, I will thank you by living as I should!
Psalm 119:7 TLB

The Benefit of God's Correction—III
Submit to Discipline

"Why did you beat your donkey those three times?" the angel of the Lord demanded. "I have come to block your way because you are stubbornly resisting me. Three times the donkey saw me and shied away; otherwise, I would certainly have killed you by now and spared the donkey."
Then Balaam confessed to the angel of the Lord, "I have sinned. I did not realize you were standing in the road to block my way. I will go back home if you are against my going."
—Numbers 22:32–34 NLT

I'm so glad to know God blocks our way when we stubbornly resist Him. His discipline is something that we need to appreciate. It would be awful if God just let us do whatever we wanted without trying to stop us and warn us. It would be as if you let a toddler run into the street whenever he wanted.

Let's be glad when God corrects us and let's be quick to repent. Submit to His discipline—it is to *your* benefit.

The "God's Correction" Challenge

- Would you believe God cared if He let you do whatever you wanted?
- Are you quick to admit when you are wrong?
- Pray that you will not resist God's correction, but instead embrace it.

The "God's Correction" Declarations

Father, your correction is always right and for my best good, that I may share your holiness. Being disciplined isn't enjoyable while it is happening—it hurts! But afterwards I can see the result, a quiet growth in grace and character.
Hebrews 12:10–11

I know it is not within my power to map my life and plan my course—so you correct me; but please be gentle.
Jeremiah 10:23–24

The Benefit of God's Defense—I
An Opportunity for Revenge

"Now's your opportunity!" David's men whispered to him. "Today is the day the Lord was talking about when he said, 'I will certainly put Saul into your power, to do with as you wish.'" Then David crept forward and cut off a piece of Saul's robe.

But then David's conscience began bothering him because he had cut Saul's robe. "The Lord knows I shouldn't have done it," he said to his men. "It is a serious thing to attack the Lord's anointed one, for the Lord himself has chosen him."

So David sharply rebuked his men and did not let them kill Saul. After Saul had left the cave and gone on his way, David came out and shouted after him, "My lord the king!" And when Saul looked around, David bowed low before him.

—1 Samuel 24:4–7 NLT

Our natural instinct is to get back at someone who wrongs us. They hit—we want to hit them back. That's why David got so much encouragement from his men to seize this opportunity against Saul.

But David knew in his spirit that he could not lay a finger on the king. David knew that he couldn't do God's job.

The "God's Defense" Challenge

- When you've been wronged, do you try to get even?
- Do you trust God to take up your case?
- List God's qualifications that make Him a better judge than you.

The "God's Defense" Declarations

Father, I will not take revenge but leave room for your wrath, for it is written: It is yours to avenge; You will repay.
Romans 12:19

I will not bear a grudge against anyone.
Leviticus 19:18

The Benefit of God's Defense—II
Proven Innocence

Then [David] shouted to Saul, "Why do you listen to the people who say I am trying to harm you? This very day you can see with your own eyes it isn't true. For the Lord placed you at my mercy back there in the cave, and some of my men told me to kill you, but I spared you. For I said, 'I will never harm him—he is the Lord's anointed one.'

"Look, my father, at what I have in my hand. It is a piece of your robe! I cut if off, but I didn't kill you. This proves that I am not trying to harm you and that I have not sinned against you, even though you have been hunting for me to kill me."
—1 Samuel 24:9–11 NLT

David was innocent. He did nothing to warrant such anger and hatred from Saul. Yet Saul hunted David, wanting to kill him.

David already knew that the Lord had chosen and anointed him to be the next king. But he was willing to let God make this happen in His time and in His way. David knew that he couldn't take the throne by force or in any unjust way. So he completely trusted God to take care of it.

The "God's Defense" Challenge

- Why is it detrimental to take justice into your own hands?
- Do you believe God is able to defend you?
- Ask God to help you with any unresolved bitterness or anger.

The "God's Defense" Declarations

Father, I will be quick to hear, slow to speak and slow to anger; for my anger does not achieve the righteousness of God.
James 1:19–20

You are my defender.
Psalm 121:5

The Benefit of God's Defense—III
The Best Defense

"The Lord will decide between us. Perhaps the Lord will punish you for what you are trying to do to me, but I will never harm you. As that old proverb says, 'From evil people come evil deeds.' So you can be sure I will never harm you.

"Who is the king of Israel trying to catch anyway? Should he spend his time chasing one who is as worthless as a dead dog or a flea? May the Lord judge which of us is right and punish the guilty one. He is my advocate, and he will rescue me from your power!"
—1 Samuel 24:12–15 NLT

David knew God as the ruler who would set things right. So, he continued to act in an upright manner toward Saul.

When we are faced with a situation where we have been unjustly treated, we must continue to do the right thing. Then evil will not get the best of us, our enemies will be at peace with us, and we will be innocent before God. God, then, is free to act.

The "God's Defense" Challenge

▸ Do you act in an upright manner when you are wronged?
▸ Why can you trust God to do what is right?
▸▸ Memorize Romans 12:12.

The "God's Defense" Declarations

Father, you are my lawyer! Plead my case! For you have redeemed my life.

You have seen the wrong they did to me; be my Judge, to prove me right.
Lamentations 3:58–59

I will strive to follow Christ's example. He never answered back when insulted; when he suffered he did not threaten to get even; he left his case in your hands, and you always judge fairly.
1 Peter 2:23

The Benefit of God's Favor—I
Hegai Is Pleased with Esther

When the king's order and edict had been proclaimed, many girls were brought to the citadel of Susa and put under the care of Hegai. Esther also was taken to the king's palace and entrusted to Hegai, who had charge of the harem. The girl pleased him and won his favor.
Immediately he provided her with her beauty treatments and special food. He assigned to her seven maids selected from the king's palace and moved her and her maids into the best place in the harem.
—Esther 2:8–9 NIV

Favor describes what those in authority want to do for someone who is subject to them. One example might be what parents want to do for their children. Or favor could be what a manager shows to his employees. When a king is pleased with his people, he wants to show special kindness to them.

Esther is a wonderful example of someone who was repeatedly shown favor. Immediately, Hegai, who was in charge of the king's harem, was pleased with Esther and took a special interest in her.

Let's remember that God delights in us because we are His. He has taken a very special interest in us.

The "God's Favor" Challenge

- Are there ways you are favorably disposed toward others?
- Do you believe that God has taken a special interest in you?
- Remember a specific time when God showed favor to you.

The "God's Favor" Declarations

Father, you show wonderful kindness to me and your favor is poured out on me because I belong to your Son. You have showered the richness of your grace down upon me.
Ephesians 1:6, 8

Surely you bless me; you surround me with your favor.
Psalm 5:12

The Benefit of God's Favor—II
Esther Wins the Favor of Everyone

When the turn came for Esther (the girl Mordecai had adopted, the daughter of his uncle Abihail) to go to the king, she asked for nothing other than what Hegai, the king's eunuch who was in charge of the harem, suggested. And Esther won the favor of everyone who saw her.

She was taken to King Xerxes in the royal residence in the tenth month, the month of Tebeth, in the seventh year of his reign.

Now the king was attracted to Esther more than to any of the other women, and she won his favor and approval more than any of the other virgins. So he set a royal crown on her head and made her queen instead of Vashti. And the king gave a great banquet, Esther's banquet, for all his nobles and officials. He proclaimed a holiday throughout the provinces and distributed gifts with royal liberality.
—Esther 2:15–18 NIV

Esther is quite a contrast to the former Queen Vashti. Queen Vashti was beautiful like Esther, but Vashti acted in ways that displeased the king. Esther won not only the Miss Susa beauty contest, but she also won the Miss Congeniality title. King Xerxes was very pleased with her.

God longs to show favor to us when we act in ways that please Him.

The "God's Favor" Challenge

- Do you win the favor of those in authority over you?
- Does your behavior warrant God's favor toward you?
- Think of a situation in which you need to ask God for favor.

The "God's Favor" Declarations

Father, you bestow favor and honor; no good thing will you withhold from me.

Psalm 84:11

You long to be gracious to me.

Isaiah 30:18

The Benefit of God's Favor—III
If It Pleases the King

"If it pleases the king," she said, "and if he regards me with favor and thinks it the right thing to do, and if he is pleased with me, let an order be written overruling the dispatches that Haman son of Hammedatha, the Agagite, devised and wrote to destroy the Jews in all the king's provinces. For how can I bear to see disaster fall on my people? How can I bear to see the destruction of my family?"

King Xerxes replied to Queen Esther and to Mordecai the Jew, "Because Haman attacked the Jews, I have given his estate to Esther, and they have hanged him on the gallows. Now write another decree in the king's name in behalf of the Jews as seems best to you, and seal it with the king's signet ring—for no document written in the king's name and sealed with his ring can be revoked."

—Esther 8:5–8 NIV

Esther bravely made a request that would affect the entire kingdom. And because King Xerxes was favorably disposed to Esther, he granted her request. As a result, Haman lost his game of hangman with Mordecai, and his evil plot to kill the Jews was foiled.

You can achieve great things with the favor of your King.

The "God's Favor" Challenge

- Do you enter God's presence with confidence?
- Do you boldly make your requests known to God?
- Consider the ways that God uses you as an example of His kindness.

The "God's Favor" Declarations

Father, you can always point to me as an example of how very rich your kindness is, as shown in all you have done for me through Jesus.

Ephesians 2:7

Your favor rests upon me.

Luke 2:14

The Benefit of God's Forgiveness—I
A "Certain" Man

So the Lord sent Nathan the prophet to tell David this story: "There were two men in a certain town. One was rich, and one was poor. The rich man owned many sheep and cattle. The poor man owned nothing but a little lamb he had worked hard to buy. He raised that little lamb, and it grew up with his children. It ate from the man's own plate and drank from his cup. He cuddled it in his arms like a baby daughter. One day a guest arrived at the home of the rich man. But instead of killing a lamb from his own flocks for food, he took the poor man's lamb and killed it and served it to his guest."

David was furious. "As surely as the Lord lives," he vowed, "any man who would do such a thing deserves to die! He must repay four lambs to the poor man for the one he stole and for having no pity."
—2 Samuel 12:1–6 NLT

The rich man in Nathan's story infuriated David. With a quick response, David determined the rich man's actions warranted death! David was a hypocrite.

It's better for the hand of God to deal with us rather than the hand of man, for God is merciful.

The "God's Forgiveness" Challenge

- Are you quick to condemn others?
- How can pausing and reflecting help you avoid being hypocritical?
- Ask the Holy Spirit to reveal sin to you; then, receive God's mercy through confession.

The "God's Forgiveness" Declarations

Father, if I conceal my sins I will not prosper, but if I confess and renounce them I will find mercy.
Proverbs 28:13

When I confess my sin, all my guilt is gone.
Psalm 32:5

The Benefit of God's Forgiveness—II
You Are That Man!

Then Nathan said to David, "You are that man! The Lord, the God of Israel, says, 'I anointed you king of Israel and saved you from the power of Saul. I gave you his house and his wives and the kingdoms of Israel and Judah. And if that had not been enough, I would have given you much, much more. Why, then, have you despised the word of the Lord and done this horrible deed? For you have murdered Uriah and stolen his wife. From this time on, the sword will be a constant threat to your family, because you have despised me by taking Uriah's wife to be your own.'"
—2 Samuel 12:7–10 NLT

David's sins were horrible. He took a life and stole a wife. God confronted David so that he would no longer conceal his sins.

God wants to bring our sins into the light where He can handle them appropriately. Satan wants to keep our sins "hidden." God convicts us to lead us to repentance. Satan heaps on us guilt and shame.

God never turns away a contrite heart and He always forgives, no matter how horrible the deed. Step into the light, and make things right!

The "God's Forgiveness" Challenge

▸ Are you hiding any sin that you need to confess?
▸ Do you believe your sin is too horrible for God to forgive?
▸▸ Become familiar with the difference between condemnation and conviction.

The "God's Forgiveness" Declarations

Father, if I confess my sins, you are faithful and just to forgive me my sins and to cleanse me from all unrighteousness.
1 John 1:9–10

You blot out my transgressions, for your own sake, and remember my sins no more.
Isaiah 43:25

The Benefit of God's Forgiveness—III
The Lord Has Forgiven You

"'Because of what you have done, I, the Lord, will cause your own household to rebel against you. I will give your wives to another man, and he will go to bed with them in public view. You did it secretly, but I will do this to you openly in the sight of all Israel.'"
Then David confessed to Nathan, "I have sinned against the Lord." Nathan replied, "Yes, but the Lord has forgiven you, and you won't die for this sin."
—2 Samuel 12:11–13 NLT

It's good that God does not treat us as our sins deserve. If He did, we wouldn't be alive to tell about it.

The down side is that sin comes with a huge price tag. David had to face some serious consequences. But once he confessed his sins, he could again face God. Everything was set right between David and his God.

If you need to set things right between you and your God, forgiveness is just a confession away.

The "God's Forgiveness" Challenge

- After God forgives, do you struggle to put sin behind you?
- Do you know that God casts your sin into the depths of the sea?
- Remember, God doesn't keep a list of your sins—He forgives and forgets.

The "God's Forgiveness" Declarations

Father, you do not treat me as my sins deserve or repay me according to my iniquities. For as high as the heavens are above the earth, so great is your love for me; as far as the east is from the west, so far have you removed my transgressions from me.
Psalm 103:10–12

You took away Satan's power to accuse me of sin, with Christ's triumph at the cross.
Colossians 2:13–15

The Benefit of God's Goodness—I
Jesus Is God's Goodness to You

In the sixth month of Elizabeth's pregnancy, God sent the angel Gabriel to Nazareth, a village in Galilee, to a virgin named Mary. She was engaged to be married to a man named Joseph, a descendant of King David. Gabriel appeared to her and said, "Greetings, favored woman! The Lord is with you!"

Confused and disturbed, Mary tried to think what the angel could mean. "Don't be frightened, Mary," the angel told her, "for God has decided to bless you! You will become pregnant and have a son, and you are to name him Jesus. He will be very great and will be called the Son of the Most High. And the Lord God will give him the throne of his ancestor David. And he will reign over Israel forever; his Kingdom will never end!"

—Luke 1:26–33 NLT

When God sent Jesus, He sent His very best. Because of this, we never need to doubt that God is good. He has only good in mind for us.

Like Mary, you might be temporarily confused by what God is doing in your life. But you will eventually come to see that His plans are always good.

The "God's Goodness" Challenge

▸ Do you ever doubt God's goodness toward you?
▸ Do you blame God for bad things that happen?
⇉ Memorize Psalm 13:6.

The "God's Goodness" Declarations

Father, since you did not spare even your own Son for me but gave him up for us all, won't you also surely give me everything else?
Romans 8:32

How great is your goodness to me. For you have stored up great blessings for me because I trust and reverence you.
Psalm 31:19

The Benefit of God's Goodness—II
Whatever God Wants

Mary asked the angel, "But how can I have a baby? I am a virgin."

The angel replied, "The Holy Spirit will come upon you, and the power of the Most High will overshadow you. So the baby born to you will be holy, and he will be called the Son of God. What's more, your relative Elizabeth has become pregnant in her old age! People used to say she was barren, but she's already in her sixth month. For nothing is impossible with God."

Mary responded, "I am the Lord's servant, and I am willing to accept whatever he wants. May everything you have said come true." And then the angel left.

—Luke 1:34–38 NLT

I'm sure Mary's wedding plans were coming along nicely when Gabriel came with some news that rocked her world. Surely her mind flooded with questions: "Why me? Will people believe me, or think me a disgrace? How will Joseph respond? Will he still want to marry me?"

But Mary's response to Gabriel settled her heart and mind. She trusted God's goodness and she accepted His plan for her.

The "God's Goodness" Challenge

▸ Has God interrupted your perfectly laid plans with a new plan?
▸ What troubling questions flood your mind about your life today?
▶▶ Tell God that you desire His will to be done in your life.

The "God's Goodness" Declarations

Father, I recall the miraculous ways you have worked in my life. Those wonderful deeds are constantly in my thoughts. I cannot stop thinking about them.

Psalm 77:11–12

Whatever is good and perfect comes to me from you, the Creator of all light, and you shine forever without change or shadow.

James 1:17

The Benefit of God's Goodness—III
Mary's Response

"Oh, how I praise the Lord. How I rejoice in God my Savior! For he took notice of his lowly servant girl, and now generation after generation will call me blessed. For he, the Mighty One, is holy and he has done great things for me. His mercy goes on from generation to generation, to all who fear him.

"His mighty arm does tremendous things! How he scatters the proud and haughty ones! He has taken princes from their thrones and exalted the lowly. He has satisfied the hungry with good things and sent the rich away with empty hands.

"And how he has helped his servant Israel! He has not forgotten his promise to be merciful. For he promised our ancestors—Abraham and his children—to be merciful to them forever."
—Luke 1:46–55 NLT

"His mighty arm does tremendous things." That statement implies that God is continually doing tremendous things.

It's important to remember all the wonderful things God has done for you. But God wants you to be excited about what's next, for the best is yet to come. You can look to the future with a big smile. God will not withhold any good thing from your life.

The "God's Goodness" Challenge

- Can you look back in your life and see the good things God has done?
- Why is it good to face the future with a smile?
- Tell someone today what tremendous things God has done for you.

The "God's Goodness" Declarations

Father, I know all that happens to me is working for my good because I love you and am fitting into your plans.
Romans 8:28

You are good, and what you do is good.
Psalm 119:68a NIV

The Benefit of God's Guidance—I
Put On Your Traveling Clothes

"Eat it with your traveling clothes on, prepared for a long journey, wearing your walking shoes and carrying your walking sticks in your hands; eat it hurriedly. This observance shall be called the Lord's Passover."

—Exodus 12:11 TLB

God led His people out of a land that had been home to them for four hundred thirty years. But God didn't just lead them; He also gave them specific instructions on how to prepare for the long journey. He wanted them in a position of readiness.

It is God's will to guide His people. It pleases Him to lead you on the right path for His name's sake. But God doesn't want to take you to places you're not yet ready to go. He always prepares you for what's next, and waits for just the right time (hopefully not four hundred thirty years!). He also wants us to be in a position of readiness so that when He gives us marching orders, we're good to go.

The "God's Guidance" Challenge

- Do you believe God wants to give you guidance?
- Over the course of your life, can you see how God prepared you for each step?
- Ask God to help you stay ready to follow His guidance.

The "God's Guidance" Declarations

Father, you teach me what is best for me, and direct me in the way I should go.

Isaiah 48:17

You are wonderful in counsel and excellent in guidance.

Isaiah 28:29

The Benefit of God's Guidance—II
No Short Cuts!

So at last Pharaoh let the people go. God did not lead them through the land of the Philistines, although that was the most direct route from Egypt to the Promised Land. The reason was that God felt the people might become discouraged by having to fight their way through, even though they had left Egypt armed; he thought they might return to Egypt. Instead, God led them along a route through the Red Sea wilderness.
—Exodus 13:17–18 TLB

Can you hear the people's reactions as Moses told them they would not be taking the most direct route to the Promised Land? They probably questioned, once again, why Moses was in charge.

But God had a good reason for leading them on an alternate route: He didn't want them to get discouraged. He knew that if they had to fight the Philistines, they might want to high tail it back to Egypt. I know if I'd been there, I would have grumbled about the leadership.

This is a great picture of how God leads His people. He doesn't know some of the variables, He knows all of them. He doesn't see part of the picture, He sees the whole picture. He doesn't see this leg of the journey, He sees the final destination.

The "God's Guidance" Challenge

- How do you react when God doesn't take the most "direct" route?
- Does it help you to know that God knows exactly where He wants to take you?
- Remember a time when you questioned God's leading, but you now clearly understand it.

The "God's Guidance" Declarations

Father, you are my God forever and ever; You will be my guide even to the end.
Psalm 48:14

You order my steps.
Proverbs 20:24

The Benefit of God's Guidance—III
Forward, March!

Then the Lord said to Moses, "Quit praying and get the people moving! Forward, march! Use your rod—hold it out over the water, and the sea will open up a path before you, and all the people of Israel shall walk through on dry ground! I will harden the hearts of the Egyptians and they will go in after you and you will see the honor I will get in defeating Pharaoh and all his armies, chariots, and horsemen. And all Egypt shall know that I am Jehovah."

Then the Angel of God, who was leading the people of Israel, moved the cloud around behind them, and it stood between the people of Israel and the Egyptians. And that night, as it changed to a pillar of fire, it gave darkness to the Egyptians but light to the people of Israel! So the Egyptians couldn't find the Israelis!

—Exodus 14:15–20 TLB

God instructed Moses to stop praying and get moving. There is a right time to pray and a right time to move. God actually wanted them to start marching forward *before* the path opened before them.

God desires to counsel you in the way you should go. But you won't necessarily have detailed marching orders before you move forward.

The "God's Guidance" Challenge

- When has God taken you to the edge of your comfort zone and said, "Go?"
- Do you pray for counsel even when you already know what to do?
- ▸▸ Obediently move forward in what God has already asked you to do.

The "God's Guidance" Declarations

Father, you guide me in the way of wisdom and lead me along straight paths.

Proverbs 4:11

You guide me with your counsel.

Psalm 73:24 NIV

The Benefit of God's Help—I
First Call for Help

Now when Daniel learned that the decree had been published, he went home to his upstairs room where the windows opened toward Jerusalem. Three times a day he got down on his knees and prayed, giving thanks to his God, just as he had done before.

Then these men went as a group and found Daniel praying and asking God for help. So they went to the king and spoke to him about his royal decree: "Did you not publish a decree that during the next thirty days anyone who prays to any god or man except to you, O king, would be thrown into the lions' den?"

The king answered, "The decree stands—in accordance with the laws of the Medes and Persians, which cannot be repealed."
—Daniel 6:10–12 NIV

This was no small problem. Daniel's disobedience to the king's decree meant his impending death. But Daniel knew exactly where he needed to be and what he needed to do. He needed to be in God's presence, on his knees in prayer, giving thanks.

That's what you need to do when you need help. Go to God first, not as a second thought, and not as a last resort. Go to God first.

The "God's Help" Challenge

- Where do you first go when you need help?
- Do you go to God with large and small problems alike?
- Commit a seemingly impossible problem to the God who can do anything.

The "God's Help" Declarations

Father, I lift up my eyes to the hills—where does my help come from? My help comes from you, the Maker of heaven and earth.
Psalm 121:1–2

You are my refuge and strength, a tested help in times of trouble.
Psalm 46:1

The Benefit of God's Help—II
He Still Lands in the Lion's Den!

Then they said to the king, "Daniel, who is one of the exiles from Judah, pays no attention to you, O king, or to the decree you put in writing. He still prays three times a day." When the king heard this, he was greatly distressed; he was determined to rescue Daniel and made every effort until sundown to save him.

Then the men went as a group to the king and said to him, "Remember, O king, that according to the law of the Medes and Persians no decree or edict that the king issues can be changed."

So the king gave the order, and they brought Daniel and threw him into the lions' den. The king said to Daniel, "May your God, whom you serve continually, rescue you!"

—Daniel 6:13–16 NIV

Sometimes we wonder why God doesn't rescue us in the way we think He should. For example, God could have found a loophole in the king's decree. Then Daniel wouldn't have to become lion chow, right?

God did want to rescue Daniel, but He wanted to do it in a way that brought Him glory. The same God that rescued Daniel wants to help you.

The "God's Help" Challenge

- Do you believe God wants to be your helper?
- What does God's help look like to you?
- Tell God you're willing for Him to rescue you in a way that brings Him glory.

The "God's Help" Declarations

Father, you want me to trust you in times of trouble, so you can rescue me and I can give you glory.

Psalm 50:15

I will call to you whenever trouble strikes, and you will help me.

Psalm 86:7 TLB

The Benefit of God's Help—III
God Sent His Angel

At the first light of dawn, the king got up and hurried to the lions' den. When he came near the den, he called to Daniel in an anguished voice, "Daniel, servant of the living God, has your God, whom you serve continually, been able to rescue you from the lions?"

Daniel answered, "O king, live forever! My God sent his angel, and he shut the mouths of the lions. They have not hurt me, because I was found innocent in his sight. Nor have I ever done any wrong before you, O king."

The king was overjoyed and gave orders to lift Daniel out of the den. And when Daniel was lifted from the den, no wound was found on him, because he had trusted in his God.

—Daniel 6:19–23 NIV

Through this dramatic rescue, God turned an entire kingdom around. King Darius proclaimed a new decree: People in every part of his kingdom must fear and reverence the God of Daniel—the living God.

The "God's Help" Challenge

- Do you give glory to God when He comes to your rescue?
- Do you believe God still uses angels to do His bidding?
- Take your eyes off your problems and focus on how big God is.

The "God's Help" Declarations

Father, when I go through deep waters and great trouble, you will be with me. When I go through rivers of difficulty, I will not drown! When I walk through the fire of oppression, I will not be burned up—the flames will not consume me. For you are the Lord my God, my Savior.

Isaiah 43:2–3

You are with me; you are my helper. I will look in triumph on my enemies.

Psalm 118:7

The Benefit of God's Love—I
The Son Went His Own Way

Then he said, "There was once a man who had two sons. The younger said to his father, 'Father, I want right now what's coming to me.'

"So the father divided the property between them. It wasn't long before the younger son packed his bags and left for a distant country. There, undisciplined and dissipated, he wasted everything he had.

"After he had gone through all his money, there was a bad famine all through that country and he began to hurt. He signed on with a citizen there who assigned him to his fields to slop the pigs. He was so hungry he would have eaten the corncobs in the pig slop, but no one would give him any."

—Luke 15:11–16

This parable is about a son who was extremely hard to love. He was demanding, undisciplined, foolish, disrespectful, and immoral. He broke his father's heart in every way imaginable.

It would have been understandable and maybe even socially acceptable if the father had disowned his son. But his love wouldn't allow it.

God's love for you is the same. There is nothing you can do to make Him love you less. Nor can anything ever separate you from His love.

The "God's Love" Challenge

- When you disappoint God, do you feel He stops loving you?
- Do you think you're a hard person for God to love?
- Pray for someone who's been hardened by life to be softened by God's love.

The "God's Love" Declarations

Father, how great is the love you have lavished on me, that I should be called your child.

1 John 3:1

I am convinced that nothing will ever separate me from your love.

Romans 8:39

The Benefit of God's Love—II
I Don't Deserve to Be Called Your Son

"That brought him to his senses. He said, 'All those farmhands working for my father sit down to three meals a day, and here I am starving to death. I'm going back to my father. I'll say to him, "Father, I've sinned against God, I've sinned before you; I don't deserve to be called your son. Take me on as a hired hand."' He got right up and went home to his father."
—Luke 15:17–20

So, the son came to his senses and wanted to return home to repent. He realized he'd made a huge mistake, and he was desperate. But returning home and saying and doing all the right things could not make his father love him more than he already did.

You can't make God love you more by doing right things. That's human love, not God's love. Human love is conditional, but God's love is unconditional. Human love is temporary, but God's love is eternal. Human love will fail you, but God's love is unfailing. You will never be loved by anyone as you are loved by God.

The "God's Love" Challenge

▸ Do you believe you need to be perfect to earn God's love?
▸ When have you been disappointed by human love?
▸▸ Meditate on God's unfailing love for you.

The "God's Love" Declarations

Father, your love stands firm forever.
Psalm 89:1

Your love is better than life.
Psalm 63:3

The Benefit of God's Love—III
A Welcome Home Party

"When he was still a long way off, his father saw him. His heart pounding, he ran out, embraced him, and kissed him. The son started his speech: 'Father, I've sinned against God, I've sinned before you; I don't deserve to be called your son ever again.'

"But the father wasn't listening. He was calling to the servants, 'Quick. Bring a clean set of clothes and dress him. Put the family ring on his finger and sandals on his feet. Then get a grain-fed heifer and roast it. We're going to feast! We're going to have a wonderful time! My son is here—given up for dead and now alive! Given up for lost and now found!' And they began to have a wonderful time."
—Luke 15:20–24

Like the father in this parable, God desires a relationship with His children. His love surpasses even that of a parent's love for a child. He is crazy about you, and he wants to lavish His love on you.

God made the ultimate demonstration of His love for you when He sent Jesus into the world to die for your sins. There is no greater love than this.

The "God's Love" Challenge

- Is your image of God's love distorted by your parents' love (or lack of) for you?
- Can you imagine how great the Father's love is for you?
- List five ways God's love has changed your life.

The "God's Love" Declarations

Father, you demonstrated your love for me in this: While I was still a sinner, Christ died for me.
Romans 5:8

Your banner over me is love.
Song of Solomon 2:4

The Benefit of God's Mercy—I
God Is Slow to Get Angry

This change of plans made Jonah very angry. He complained to the Lord about it: "This is exactly what I thought you'd do, Lord, when I was there in my own country and you first told me to come here. That's why I ran away to Tarshish. For I knew you were a gracious God, merciful, slow to get angry, and full of kindness; I knew how easily you could cancel your plans for destroying these people.

"Please kill me, Lord; I'd rather be dead than alive [when nothing that I told them happens]." Then the Lord said, "Is it right to be angry about this?"

—Jonah 4:1–4 TLB

When God asked Jonah to go to Nineveh, he willfully refused and took a one hundred eighty degree turn to Tarshish.

It was a good thing for Jonah that God is the God of second chances. God mercifully spared Jonah from the grave by sending a big fish to swallow him. Only then was Jonah ready to obey the word of the Lord.

God is consistent and shows no partiality. God's heart was tender toward Jonah, the people of Nineveh, and His heart is tender toward you.

The "God's Mercy" Challenge

- When is it hard for you to accept that God is tender and merciful toward you?
- Do you believe that God is the God of second chances?
- Reflect on a time when God showed you His tender mercy.

The "God's Mercy" Declarations

Father, your steadfast love never ceases, your mercies never come to an end; they are new every morning; great is your faithfulness.
Lamentations 3:22–23

As a father is tender and sympathetic to his children, so you are to me.
Psalm 103:13

The Benefit of God's Mercy—II
The People of Nineveh Repent

So Jonah went out and sat sulking on the east side of the city, and he made a leafy shelter to shade him as he waited there to see if anything would happen to the city. And when the leaves of the shelter withered in the heat, the Lord arranged for a vine to grow up quickly and spread its broad leaves over Jonah's head to shade him. This made him comfortable and very grateful.

But God also prepared a worm! The next morning the worm ate through the stem of the plant, so that it withered away and died.
—Jonah 4:5–7 TLB

Jonah just didn't get it. It almost seems that he wanted to grab a bucket of popcorn, sit on the hillside, and watch God torch the people.

But God sent him to Nineveh to warn the people so that they might repent and be saved, not destroyed. So, Jonah warned the people of God's impending judgment and destruction. To God's delight, the people listened and turned from their evil ways.

God is not willing that anyone should perish. He wants to give people every possible chance to be reconciled to Him.

The "God's Mercy" Challenge

- Do you know the compassionate side of God?
- Do you genuinely desire God's mercy for all people?
- Demonstrate God's tender mercy to someone today.

The "God's Mercy" Declarations

Father, you are a compassionate and gracious God, slow to anger, abounding in love and faithfulness, maintaining love to thousands, and forgiving my wickedness, rebellion and sin.
Exodus 34:6–7

You long to be gracious to me; You rise to show me compassion.
Isaiah 30:18

The Benefit of God's Mercy—III
God Longs to Show Mercy

Then, when the sun was hot, God ordered a scorching east wind to blow on Jonah, and the sun beat down upon his head until he grew faint and wished to die. For he said, "Death is better than this!"
And God said to Jonah, "Is it right for you to be angry because the plant died?"
"Yes," Jonah said, "it is; it is right for me to be angry enough to die!"
Then the Lord said, "You feel sorry for yourself when your shelter is destroyed, though you did no work to put it there, and it is, at best, short-lived. And why shouldn't I feel sorry for a great city like Nineveh with its 120,000 people in utter spiritual darkness, and all its cattle?"
—Jonah 4:8–11 TLB

Jonah had a huge mood swing over a plant! God had a change of heart about the people He loved. They wanted to change their evil ways and He rejoiced.

God must judge sin because He is holy, but He must show mercy because of His great love. How did He do that for you? He did it through the cross. In Jesus, God's justice and mercy were perfectly satisfied.

The "God's Mercy" Challenge

- Does God want anyone to live in spiritual darkness?
- Do you view God only as your judge?
- ▸▸ Consider how the cross satisfied God's need to show justice and mercy.

The "God's Mercy" Declarations

Father, you have not dealt with me according to my sins, nor punished me according to my iniquities. For as the heavens are high above the earth, so great is your mercy toward me.
Psalm 103:10–11

You are gracious and righteous, full of compassion.
Psalm 116:5

The Benefit of God's Peace—I
The Beginning of Peace

> *So now, since we have been made right in God's sight by faith in his promises, we can have real peace with him because of what Jesus Christ our Lord has done for us. For because of our faith, he has brought us into this place of highest privilege where we now stand, and we confidently and joyfully look forward to actually becoming all that God has had in mind for us to be.*
> —Romans 5:1–2 TLB

You cannot experience true peace until you are right with God. Before being made right, you were unsettled—even if you were unaware of it—about God, your life, and death.

God sent Jesus, the Prince of Peace, into your world so you could have the relationship with God you were created to have. When Christ took up residence in your heart, He brought peace with Him. And nothing can take that peace away.

All is well with God and you. Now that, my friend, is the beginning of peace.

The "God's Peace" Challenge

- Can anything take your God-given peace away?
- Do you try to find peace from a source other than God?
- Make certain you have a relationship with the Prince of Peace.

The "God's Peace" Declarations

Father, you gave me a gift—peace of mind and heart! And the peace you give isn't fragile like the peace the world gives. So I won't be troubled or afraid.
John 14:27

Since I have been justified through faith, I have peace with you through Jesus.
Romans 5:1

The Benefit of God's Peace—II
Don't You Care If We Perish?

On that day, when evening had come, he said to them, "Let us go across to the other side." And leaving the crowd, they took him with them in the boat, just as he was. And other boats were with him. And a great storm of wind arose, and the waves beat into the boat, so that the boat was already filling. But he was in the stern, asleep on the cushion; and they woke him and said to him, "Teacher, do you not care if we perish?"
—Mark 4:35–38 RSV

In their storm-tossed anxiety, the disciples questioned if Jesus cared whether they lived or died. They had witnessed His miraculous power many times and they'd seen His great compassion for people. Yet they still questioned. Meanwhile, Jesus, not having a care in the world, slept like a baby in the stern of the storm-tossed boat.

We're no different from the disciples. We've seen God move in our lives in powerful ways and we know how deeply He loves us. Yet, we still question Him: "Don't you care? Why aren't You doing anything?"

God does care about you, and He's got you covered.

The "God's Peace" Challenge

- Do you ever question if Jesus cares about your problems?
- Do you anxiously struggle with the problems in your life?
- Reflect on a stormy time when you experienced God's peace and power.

The "God's Peace" Declarations

Father, I will let you have all my worries and cares, for you are always thinking about me and watching everything that concerns me.
1 Peter 5:7

You will keep me in perfect peace when my mind is stayed on you, because I trust in you.
Isaiah 26:3

The Benefit of God's Peace—III
Peace! Be Still!

And he awoke and rebuked the wind, and said to the sea, "Peace! Be still!" And the wind ceased, and there was a great calm. He said to them, "Why are you afraid? Have you no faith?" And they were filled with awe, and said to one another, "Who then is this, that even wind and sea obey him?"

—Mark 4:39–41 RSV

Jesus has a calming effect on storms and people. In this particular case, He quieted the storm. But whether or not He calms the storms around you, He wants to calm you. He makes it possible for you to have peace, even when the winds of adversity swirl around you.

When you choose to worry, you forfeit God's peace. He wants to know what concerns you, so cast your cares on Him, pray about everything, and don't be anxious about anything. Then His peace will guard your heart and mind.

The "God's Peace" Challenge

- Do you get discouraged when God doesn't calm the storms in your life?
- How can you have a sense of peace in the midst of storms?
- Write a prayer to God, giving Him all your worries.

The "God's Peace" Declarations

Father, I will not fret or worry. Instead of worrying, I will pray. I will let my petitions and praises shape my worries into prayers, letting you know my concerns. And before I know it, a sense of your wholeness, everything coming together for good, will come and settle me down. It is wonderful what happens when Christ displaces worry at the center of my life.

Philippians 4:6–7

I will lie down and sleep in peace, for you alone, make me dwell in safety.

Psalm 4:8

The Benefit of God's Presence—I
They Lost Their Best Friend

That same day two of them were walking to the village Emmaus, about seven miles out of Jerusalem. They were deep in conversation, going over all these things that had happened. In the middle of their talk and questions, Jesus came up and walked along with them. But they were not able to recognize who he was.

He asked, "What's this you're discussing so intently as you walk along?"

They just stood there, long-faced, like they had lost their best friend.

—Luke 24:13–17

These were tough days for the followers of Christ. The One they thought would deliver them had been betrayed, beaten, and crucified. Now it seemed all their hopes were dashed. They'd spent so much time with Jesus, learned from Him, grew to love Him. Now He was gone. They really did lose their best friend—temporarily.

It was the day of Jesus' resurrection when He met these two on the road to Emmaus. Jesus was walking with them and they just didn't recognize Him.

Jesus died for you so He wouldn't have to live without you. He is with you—even when you can't recognize His presence.

The "God's Presence" Challenge

- How do you feel knowing Jesus doesn't want to live without you?
- Do you ever feel alone?
- Ask God to help you recognize His presence as you walk through your day.

The "God's Presence" Declarations

Father, I can be sure that you are with me always, even to the end of the world.

Matthew 28:20

As I come near to you, you will come near to me.

James 4:8

The Benefit of God's Presence—II
Another Friend!

"I [Jesus] will talk to the Father, and he'll provide you another Friend so that you will always have someone with you. This Friend is the Spirit of Truth. The godless world can't take him in because it doesn't have eyes to see him, doesn't know what to look for. But you know him already because he has been staying with you, and will even be in you!

"I will not leave you orphaned. I'm coming back. In just a little while the world will no longer see me, but you're going to see me because I am alive and you're about to come alive."
—John 14:15–19

Jesus didn't want to leave His followers orphaned. Before this time, the Jews' only concept of God's Presence was of His distance from them. God's Presence was sacred and unapproachable. It was a Presence that only the few and the chosen could know.

Jesus announced a new way. God wanted to pour His Spirit on His sons and daughters. He wanted to be present with His people in a personal way.

Now, He wants to be close to you. He didn't just move into your neighborhood, He moved into your house—permanently.

The "God's Presence" Challenge

- Did you come to life when God's Spirit moved in?
- Can you see the evidence of God's Spirit in your life?
- Memorize Luke 11:13.

The "God's Presence" Declarations

Father, I am your temple and your Spirit lives in me.
1 Corinthians 3:16

You will never desert me, nor will you ever forsake me.
Hebrews 13:5–6

The Benefit of God's Presence—III
The Holy Spirit

"But you will receive power when the Holy Spirit comes on you; and you will be my witnesses in Jerusalem, and in all Judea and Samaria, and to the ends of the earth."
—Acts 1:8 NIV

This Scripture says that you *will* receive power when the Holy Spirit comes on you, not you *might*. This verse also says you *will* be my witnesses, not you *might*. You are now a Holy Spirit filled and empowered child of the living God. You are one of God's Official Mobilization Units. He can use you to affect His world in a unique way.

You are Jesus with skin on He can use you to advance His kingdom. You can be His hands to serve the needy. You can be His feet to bring His good news to those who have yet to hear.

Wherever you go, you take His presence and His power with you.

The "God's Presence" Challenge

▸ Are you making use of the Spirit's power in your life?
▸ Do you believe the same Spirit that raised Christ from the dead dwells in you?
▶ Ask God to fill you with His Holy Spirit now.

The "God's Presence" Declarations

Father, the same Spirit that raised Christ from the dead now dwells in me.
Romans 8:11

Your nearness is my good.
Psalm 73:28

The Benefit of God's Protection—I
What You Whisper in Your Bedroom

One time when the king of Aram was at war with Israel, after consulting with his officers, he said, "At such and such a place I want an ambush set."

The Holy Man sent a message to the king of Israel: "Watch out when you're passing this place, because Aram has set an ambush there."

So the king of Israel sent word concerning the place of which the Holy Man had warned him.

This kind of thing happened all the time.

The king of Aram was furious over all this. He called his officers together and said, "Tell me, who is leaking information to the king of Israel? Who is the spy in our ranks?"

But one of his men said, "No, my master, dear king. It's not any of us. It's Elisha the prophet in Israel. He tells the king of Israel everything you say, even what you whisper in your bedroom."

—2 Kings 6:8–12

Scripture tells many ways that God protects His people. In this instance, God revealed vital information to the king of Israel that saved his life. God continues to caution His people today. Listen to the Spirit's promptings.

The "God's Protection" Challenge

- Have you ever ignored a warning from the Holy Spirit, and regretted it?
- Do you believe God wants to protect you, even as a parent protects a child?
- Think of a time when you responded to God's warning of danger.

The "God's Protection" Declarations

Father, you will keep me from all harm—you will watch over my life; you will watch over my coming and going both now and forevermore.

Psalm 121:7–8

You are a shield around me.

Psalm 3:3

The Benefit of God's Protection—II
We're Surrounded!

The king said, "Go and find out where he is. I'll send someone and capture him."

The report came back, "He's in Dothan."

Then he dispatched horses and chariots, an impressive fighting force. They came by night and surrounded the city.

Early in the morning a servant of the Holy Man got up and went out. Surprise! Horses and chariots surrounding the city! The young man exclaimed, "Oh, master! What shall we do?"

He said, "Don't worry about it—there are more on our side than on their side."

Then Elisha prayed: "O God, open his eyes and let him see."

The eyes of the young man were opened and he saw. A wonder! The whole mountainside full of horses and chariots of fire surrounding Elisha!

—2 Kings 6:13–15

It's good to know that God is never caught off guard, as was Elisha's servant. He knew they couldn't defend themselves, and the situation seemed impossible to escape. But God made a way when there seemed to be no way.

When it feels as if your enemies are closing in on you, remember that God is your protector. He is greater than anything or anyone that comes against you. He wants to keep you out of harm's way, and He has the ability to do it.

The "God's Protection" Challenge

- What can harm you if God is protecting you?
- Do you believe that God has the resources to protect you?
- Ask God to open your eyes to see His protection all around you.

The "God's Protection" Declarations

Father, you are my rock, my fortress and my deliverer; my God, in whom I take refuge.

Psalm 18:2

You are my hiding place; you will protect me from trouble.

Psalm 32:7

The Benefit of God's Protection—III
Your Armor

So take everything the Master has set out for you, well-made weapons of the best materials. And put them to use so you will be able to stand up to everything the Devil throws your way. This is no afternoon athletic contest that we'll walk away from and forget about in a couple of hours. This is for keeps, a life-or-death fight to the finish against the Devil and all his angels.

Be prepared. You're up against far more than you can handle on your own. Take all the help you can get, every weapon God has issued, so that when it's all over but the shouting you'll still be on your feet. Truth, righteousness, peace, faith, and salvation are more than words. Learn how to apply them. You'll need them throughout your life.

God's Word is an indispensable weapon. In the same way, prayer is essential in this ongoing warfare. Pray hard and long. Pray for your brothers and sisters. Keep your eyes open. Keep each other's spirits up so that no one falls behind or drops out.
—Ephesians 6:10–18

God gave you armor and weapons for your protection, but you have the responsibility to use them. You have a real enemy who wars against you. Stay alert and cover others so there aren't any casualties.

The "God's Protection" Challenge

- Are you covering others with prayers of protection?
- Why do you need protection from the devil?
- Stand firmly against the enemy by using every weapon that God gives you.

The "God's Protection" Declarations

Father, your name is a strong tower; I can run into it and be safe.
Proverbs 18:10

The evil one cannot harm me.
1 John 5:18

The Benefit of God's Provision—I
Your Provider

Then Elijah, the prophet from Tishbe in Gilead, told King Ahab, "As surely as the Lord God of Israel lives—the God whom I worship and serve—there won't be any dew or rain for several years until I say the word!"

Then the Lord said to Elijah, "Go to the east and hide by Cherith Brook at a place east of where it enters the Jordan River. Drink from the brook and eat what the ravens bring you, for I have commanded them to feed you."

So he did as the Lord had told him to, and camped beside the brook. The ravens brought him bread and meat each morning and evening, and he drank from the brook. But after awhile the brook dried up, for there was no rainfall anywhere in the land.
—1 Kings 17:1–7 TLB

Even in the midst of a drought, God provided for Elijah. The ravens personally delivered even his food to him. It's God's job to provide for you out of His limitless resources. And because of that, there will never be any disparity between your needs and God's desire and ability to meet them.

The "God's Provision" Challenge

- ▸ Do you think God knows, even more than you do, what you need?
- ▸ If God has unlimited resources, do you believe He'll meet your needs?
- ▸▸ List three ways God has provided for your needs this month.

The "God's Provision" Declarations

Father, you are able to make all grace abound to me, so that in all things at all times, having all that I need, I will abound in every good work.
2 Corinthians 9:8

You know what I need before I even ask.
Matthew 6:8

The Benefit of God's Provision—II
Last Meal

Then the Lord said to him, "Go and live in the village of Zarephath, near the city of Sidon. There is a widow there who will feed you. I have given her my instructions."

So he went to Zarephath. As he arrived at the gates of the city he saw a widow gathering sticks; and he asked her for a cup of water.

As she was going to get it, he called to her, "Bring me a bite of bread, too."

But she said, "I swear by the Lord your God that I haven't a single piece of bread in the house. And I have only a handful of flour left and a little cooking oil in the bottom of the jar. I was just gathering a few sticks to cook this last meal, and then my son and I must die of starvation."
—1 Kings 17:8–12 TLB

Why would God choose a widow who was down to her last meal to provide for Elijah? God's ways are higher than our ways, so we don't always understand what He's up to.

As humans, we like to settle into predictable patterns. We think God will provide for us in one way when He might have something completely different in mind.

The "God's Provision" Challenge

▸ Do you recognize God's provision for you?
▸ Do you limit God to your ideas and methods of provision?
▸▸ Memorize Isaiah 55:9.

The "God's Provision" Declarations

Father, you made the world and everything in it and you give me life, breath, and satisfy my every need.
Acts 17:24–26

You will meet all my needs according to your glorious riches in Christ Jesus.
Philippians 4:19

The Benefit of God's Provision—III
A Supply That Won't Run Dry

But Elijah said to her, "Don't be afraid! Go ahead and cook that 'last meal,' but bake me a little loaf of bread first; and afterwards there will still be enough food for you and your son. For the Lord God of Israel says that there will always be plenty of flour and oil left in your containers until the time when the Lord sends rain, and the crops grow again!"

So she did as Elijah said, and she and Elijah and her son continued to eat from her supply of flour and oil as long as it was needed. For no matter how much they used, there was always plenty left in the containers, just as the Lord had promised through Elijah!
—1 Kings 17:13–16 TLB

At first, the widow fussed about starving to death, but God gave her a supply that would not run dry.

You never have to be concerned about your needs being met. God will never have to file for bankruptcy. Out of His bounty, God will meet your physical, emotional, spiritual, financial, and relational needs. And with God, there will always be plenty to go around.

The "God's Provision" Challenge

- Are you afraid that God's supply to you will run dry?
- Why is God best suited to supply what is lacking in your life right now?
- Make your needs known to God, and leave the rest to Him.

The "God's Provision" Declarations

Father, your divine power has given me everything I need for life and godliness.
2 Peter 1:3

As I honor you with my increase, my barns will be filled to overflowing.
Proverbs 3:9–10

The Benefit of God's Righteousness—I
You Are Declared Righteous

Abraham was, humanly speaking, the founder of our Jewish nation. What were his experiences concerning this question of being saved by faith? Was it because of his good deeds that God accepted him? If so, he would have had something to boast about. But from God's point of view Abraham had no basis at all for pride. For the Scriptures tell us, "Abraham believed God, so God declared him to be righteous."

When people work, their wages are not a gift. Workers earn what they receive. But people are declared righteous because of their faith, not because of their work.
—Romans 4:1–5 NLT

Abraham, like us, was far from perfect. When he feared man and was under pressure, he told falsehoods. His son Isaac and grandson Jacob did the same thing. Yet, Abraham was declared to be right before God. Why? He trusted God to set him right. The same is true for you. Because of your faith, God declares you righteous.

The "God's Righteousness" Challenge

▸ Are you trying to be accepted by God through your good works?
▸ Why does God declare you righteous by faith alone?
▸▸ Trust God alone to set you right.

The "God's Righteousness" Declarations

Father, I have been crucified with Christ and I no longer live, but Christ lives in me. The life I live in the body, I live by faith in your Son, who loved me and gave himself for me. I do not set aside your grace, for if righteousness could be gained through the law, Christ died for nothing!
Galatians 2:20–21

I will wear the breastplate of righteousness, knowing I have your approval.
Ephesians 6:14

The Benefit of God's Righteousness—II
You Can't Earn God's Acceptance

King David spoke of this, describing the happiness of an undeserving sinner who is declared to be righteous: "Oh, what joy for those whose disobedience is forgiven, whose sins are put out of sight. Yes, what joy for those whose sin is no longer counted against them by the Lord."

Now then, is this blessing only for the Jews, or is it for Gentiles, too? Well, what about Abraham? We have been saying he was declared righteous by God because of his faith. But how did his faith help him? Was he declared righteous only after he had been circumcised, or was it before he was circumcised? The answer is that God accepted him first, and then he was circumcised later!

—Romans 4:6–10 NLT

Through personal experience, David knew how wonderful it felt to be declared righteous even though he didn't deserve it. Even King David couldn't get it right all of the time.

After you give your heart to Christ and are declared righteous, you still make mistakes. God knows you can't get it one hundred percent right, one hundred percent of the time. It's impossible for you to earn God's acceptance by your own goodness.

The "God's Righteousness" Challenge

- Do you think you have to earn God's acceptance?
- Are you relieved to know that King David sinned, that he didn't always get it right?
- Memorize Ephesians 2:8–9.

The "God's Righteousness" Declarations

Father, you put my wrong on Christ, who never did anything wrong, so I could be put right with you.

2 Corinthians 5:21

Christ bore my sins so that I can be free to live the right way.

1 Peter 2:24

The Benefit of God's Righteousness—III
Ceremonies Don't Make You Right

The circumcision ceremony was a sign that Abraham already had faith and that God had already accepted him and declared him to be righteous—even before he was circumcised. So Abraham is the spiritual father of those who have faith but have not been circumcised. They are made right with God by faith.

And Abraham is also the spiritual father of those who have been circumcised, but only if they have the same kind of faith Abraham had before he was circumcised.

—Romans 4:11–12 NLT

Sometimes people get the idea that if they go through all the right religious, ceremonial "hoops," they will be right before God.

Ceremonies are a great way to outwardly express your faith relationship with God. But they are powerless to make you righteous. You are made right by your faith in Christ, period.

The "God's Righteousness" Challenge

- Do you avoid ceremonies because you see them as unnecessary?
- Do you demand ceremonies from others that God doesn't demand from them?
- Evaluate the significance that ceremonies have in your life.

The "God's Righteousness" Declarations

Father, I have put aside all else, counting it worth less than nothing, in order that I can have Christ, and become one with him, no longer counting on being saved by being good enough or by obeying your laws, but by trusting Christ to save me; for your way of making me right with yourself depends on my faith—counting on Christ alone.

Philippians 3:9

Like Abraham, I am declared right with you because of my faith. But my faith is made complete as I live out what I believe.

James 2:21–22

The Benefit of God's Strength—I
Your Own Strength

The Lord then said to Gideon, "There are too many of you! I can't let all of you fight the Midianites, for then the people of Israel will boast to me that they saved themselves by their own strength! Send home any of your men who are timid and frightened."

So twenty-two thousand of them left, and only ten thousand remained who were willing to fight.

But the Lord told Gideon, "There are still too many! Bring them down to the spring and I'll show you which ones shall go with you and which ones shall not."

So Gideon assembled them at the water. There the Lord told him, "Divide them into two groups decided by the way they drink. In Group 1 will be all the men who cup the water in their hands to get it to their mouths and lap it like dogs. In Group 2 will be those who kneel, with their mouths in the stream."

—Judges 7:2–5 TLB

God knew that Gideon's army would want to take credit for victory over the Midianites. I hate to break it to you, but God is not impressed with your strength. God delights to show Himself strong on your behalf.

The "God's Strength" Challenge

- Do you try to impress God and others with your own strength?
- Do you allow God to show Himself strong on your behalf?
- Confess to God if you've depended on your own strength, and not on His.

The "God's Strength" Declarations

Father, my flesh and my heart fail; But you are the strength of my heart and my portion forever.

Psalm 73:26

Your eyes range throughout the earth to strengthen those whose hearts are fully committed to you.

2 Chronicles 16:9

The Benefit of God's Strength—II
The Runt of the Litter

Only three hundred of the men drank from their hands; all the others drank with their mouths to the stream.
"I'll conquer the Midianites with these three hundred!" the Lord told Gideon. "Send all the others home!"
So after Gideon had collected all the clay jars and trumpets they had among them, he sent them home, leaving only three hundred men with him.
During the night, with the Midianites camped in the valley just below, the Lord said to Gideon, "Get up! Take your troops and attack the Midianites, for I will cause you to defeat them!"
—Judges 7:6–9 TLB

Gideon's initial response to God's call to save Israel from Midian was one of inadequacy. He was from the weakest clan in Manasseh, and to top it off, he was the runt of the litter. Now God had pared down Gideon's army to only three hundred men. God did not need human strength or a large army to defeat the Midianites.

God needs people who are willing to be used—even in their weakness. When you are weak, God is strong. God will help you go far beyond where your own strength can take you.

The "God's Strength" Challenge

- Do you ever use your weaknesses as an excuse to not obey God's call?
- Do you let your inadequacies limit what you are willing to do for God?
- Think of a time when God strengthened you beyond your human ability.

The "God's Strength" Declarations

Father, you give me strength when I am weary and increase the power when I am weak.
Isaiah 40:29

You are my strength and my song; you are my salvation.
Psalm 118:14

The Benefit of God's Strength—III
God's Might!

It was just after midnight and the change of guards when Gideon and the hundred men with him crept to the outer edge of the camp of Midian.
Suddenly they blew their trumpets and broke their clay jars so that their torches blazed into the night. Then the other two hundred of his men did the same, blowing the trumpets in their right hands, and holding the flaming torches in their left hands, all yelling, "For the Lord and for Gideon!"
Then they just stood and watched as the whole vast enemy army began rushing around in a panic, shouting and running away. For in the confusion the Lord caused the enemy troops to begin fighting and killing each other from one end of the camp to the other, and they fled into the night to places as far away as Beth-shittah near Zererah, and to the border of Abel-meholah near Tabbath.
—Judges 7:19–22 TLB

You might think God would choose the brightest, richest, best-looking, fastest, strongest achievers to get His work done. But God does not regard us for our strengths or despise us for our weaknesses. He uses ordinary folks to show the world how extraordinary He is.

The "God's Strength" Challenge

- Do you think you can accomplish great things for God in your own might?
- Do you know that you can do all things through Christ who strengthens you?
- Ask God to strengthen you to perform a task that seems overwhelming.

The "God's Strength" Declarations

Father, I can do everything you ask me to with the help of Christ who gives me the strength and power.
Philippians 4:13

I will be strong in the Lord and in his mighty power.
Ephesians 6:10

The Benefit of God's Word—I
A Good Weed N' Feed Program

Next Jesus was taken into the wild by the Spirit for the Test. The Devil was ready to give it. Jesus prepared for the Test by fasting forty days and forty nights. That left him, of course, in a state of extreme hunger, which the Devil took advantage of in the first test: "Since you are God's Son, speak the word that will turn these stones into loaves of bread."

Jesus answered by quoting Deuteronomy: "It takes more than bread to stay alive. It takes a steady stream of words from God's mouth."

—Matthew 4:1–4

Because Jesus was at the point of extreme physical need, the devil knew He was vulnerable to temptation. But Jesus knew where to find the power to fight the devil. It was in God's Word, which is an indispensable weapon in the life of a believer.

And we need a steady diet of God's Word to nourish and equip our spirits and to kill all the weeds that spring up, weeds such as lies, temptations, doubts, fears, and anything else that interferes with our spiritual health, pulling us away from God.

The "God's Word" Challenge

- Are you aware of the power that exists in God's Word?
- Do you use God's Word to get rid of the weeds in your life?
- Make a commitment to feed your spirit with God's Word every day.

The "God's Word" Declarations

Father, your word that goes out from your mouth will not return to you empty, but will accomplish what you desire and achieve the purpose for which you sent it.

Isaiah 55:11

I have hidden your word in my heart that I might not sin against you.

Psalm 119:11 NIV

The Benefit of God's Word—II
God's Word Is Alive and Active

For the second test the Devil took him to the Holy City. He sat him on top of the Temple and said, "Since you are God's Son, jump." The Devil goaded him by quoting Psalm 91: "He has placed you in the care of angels. They will catch you so that you won't so much as stub your toe on a stone."

Jesus countered with another citation from Deuteronomy: "Don't you dare test the Lord your God."

—Matthew 4:5–7

Jesus didn't see God's Word as dead historical information. God's Word was alive and active in the life of Jesus. Because of this, He saw right through the devil's temptation.

The devil took a portion of God's Word and distorted it. He did that with Eve and with Jesus, and he continues to twist God's Word today.

The devil is the father of all lies and is a cunning snake. God's Word is Truth. We need God's Word to be alive and active in our lives so that we have the knowledge to distinguish the devil's lies from God's Truth.

The "God's Word" Challenge

- Do you see God's Word as one hundred percent Truth?
- Are you able to distinguish the devil's lies from God's Truth?
- Ask God to make His Word alive in your heart so you can know the Truth.

The "God's Word" Declarations

Father, your word is living and active. Sharper than any double-edged sword, it penetrates even to dividing soul and spirit, joints and marrow; it judges the thoughts and attitudes of my heart.

Hebrews 4:12–13

I delight in your decrees; I will not neglect your word.

Psalm 119:16 NIV

The Benefit of God's Word—III
Jesus Obeyed God's Word

For the third test, the Devil took him on the peak of a huge mountain. He gestured expansively, pointing out all the earth's kingdoms, how glorious they all were. Then he said, "They're yours—lock, stock, and barrel. Just go down on your knees and worship me, and they're yours."

Jesus' refusal was curt: "Beat it, Satan!" He backed his rebuke with a third quotation from Deuteronomy: "Worship the Lord your God, and only him. Serve him with absolute single-heartedness."

The Test was over. The Devil left. And in his place, angels! Angels came and took care of Jesus' needs.
—Matthew 4:8–11

This time the devil tried to offer Jesus yet another cheap counterfeit. He tried to get Jesus to bail on God's plan by taking over the world! But Jesus didn't just preach God's Word—He lived it.

We need to do the same. When you obey God's Word, you build a solid foundation in your life and nothing can shake you.

If you want to experience the power of God's Word in your life, then practice what you preach.

The "God's Word" Challenge

- Are you presently deceived by any of the devil's cheap counterfeits?
- Do you let God's Word go in one ear and out the other?
- Find an accountability partner to help ensure you're applying God's Word.

The "God's Word" Declarations

Father, as I hear your words and put them into practice, I will be like a wise man that built his house on the rock.
Matthew 7:24

I will never forget your precepts, for by them you have preserved my life.
Psalm 119:93 NIV

The Benefit of Good Judgment—I
Abigail Takes Action

When Abigail saw David, she quickly got off her donkey and bowed down before David with her face to the ground. She fell at his feet and said: "My lord, let the blame be on me alone. Please let your servant speak to you; hear what your servant has to say. May my lord pay no attention to that wicked man Nabal. He is just like his name—his name is Fool, and folly goes with him. But as for me, your servant, I did not see the men my master sent.

"Now since the Lord has kept you, my master, from bloodshed and from avenging yourself with your own hands, as surely as the Lord lives and as you live, may your enemies and all who intend to harm my master be like Nabal. And let this gift, which your servant has brought to my master, be given to the men who follow you."
—1 Samuel 25:23–27 NIV

Abigail's husband, Nabal, responded rudely to David's request for hospitality. When Abigail was told about the incident, she knew immediately what she needed to do. She discerned that her entire household was in terrible trouble if she didn't take action.

God gave Abigail good judgment so that she could meet with David and diffuse his anger.

The "Good Judgment" Challenge

- Are you able to give the right response in a difficult situation?
- Do you sometimes see things that aren't apparent to others?
- Reflect on a time when God gave you good judgment.

The "Good Judgment" Declarations

Father, as I preserve sound judgment and discernment, and keep them in sight, they will be life for me.
Proverbs 3:21–22

Discretion will protect me, and understanding will guard me.
Proverbs 2:11

The Benefit of Good Judgment—II
The Heart of the Matter

"Please forgive your servant's offense, for the Lord will certainly make a lasting dynasty for my master, because he fights the Lord's battles. Let no wrongdoing be found in you as long as you live. Even though someone is pursuing you to take your life, the life of my master will be bound securely in the bundle of the living by the Lord your God. But the lives of your enemies he will hurl away as from the pocket of a sling.

"When the Lord has done for my master every good thing he promised concerning him and has appointed him leader over Israel, my master will not have on his conscience the staggering burden of needless bloodshed or of having avenged himself. And when the Lord has brought my master success, remember your servant."
—1 Samuel 25:28–31 NIV

Abigail cut right to the heart of this potentially explosive situation. Amazingly, she said the exact words David needed to hear.

God can help you get to the heart of a matter and he knows exactly what to say and do.

The "Good Judgment" Challenge

▸ Are you facing circumstances that require good judgment?
▸ When have you been able to cut to the heart of a matter?
▸▸ Ask God for words fitly spoken in all circumstances.

The "Good Judgment" Declarations

Father, as you help me to grow in knowledge and depth of insight, I will be able to discern what is best and be pure and blameless until the day of Christ.
Philippians 1:9–10

By constant use of your Word, I will be trained to distinguish good from evil.
Hebrews 5:14

The Benefit of Good Judgment—III
Many Are Blessed Because of Good Judgment

David said to Abigail, "Praise be to the Lord, the God of Israel, who has sent you today to meet me. May you be blessed for your good judgment and for keeping me from bloodshed this day and from avenging myself with my own hands. Otherwise, as surely as the Lord, the God of Israel, lives, who has kept me from harming you, if you had not come quickly to meet me, not one male belonging to Nabal would have been left alive by daybreak."

Then David accepted from her hand what she had brought him and said, "Go home in peace. I have heard your words and granted your request."

—1 Samuel 25:32–35 NIV

If not for Abigail's good judgment, every male belonging to Nabal would have been killed. David would have been guilty of getting even with Nabal by shedding innocent blood. And God would not have been pleased with David. Abigail saved the day.

The "Good Judgment" Challenge

- Has good judgment kept you from harm's way?
- How might God benefit when you use good judgment?
- Pray for God's discernment in any decision you face today.

The "Good Judgment" Declarations

Father, you grant wisdom! Your every word is a treasure of knowledge and understanding. You grant good sense to me. You are my shield, protecting me and guarding my pathway. You show me how to distinguish right from wrong, how to find the right decision every time.

Proverbs 2:6–9

I will be happier than a man who is immensely rich when I know right from wrong and have good judgment and common sense.

Proverbs 3:13–14

The Benefit of Healing—I
She Heard About Jesus

A woman who had suffered a condition of hemorrhaging for twelve years—a long succession of physicians had treated her, and treated her badly, taking all her money and leaving her worse off than before—had heard about Jesus. She slipped in from behind and touched his robe. She was thinking to herself, "If I can put a finger on his robe, I can get well."
—Mark 5:25–27

Jesus had a reputation for making people well. That's why crowds always surrounded Him and people pressed in to touch Him. Unlike the physicians who had disappointed this woman, Jesus never disappointed anyone who sought Him for healing.

The woman knew Jesus had a one hundred percent success rate. She had suffered for twelve long years and only grew worse, exhausting all her options. She was desperate to be healed.

God's best intentions are for our healing and wholeness—spiritually, emotionally, and physically. That's why we have such a strong, God-given desire to be healed. So, asking God for healing in any area of our lives is completely appropriate.

God is the Great Physician—He is the source of all healing.

The "Healing" Challenge

▸ Do you believe God gives you the desire to be healed?
▸ Where do you go when you need healing?
▶▶ Consider why God is the ultimate source of healing.

The "Healing" Declarations

Father, you were pierced for my transgressions, you were crushed for my iniquities; the punishment that brought my peace was upon you, and by your wounds, I am healed.
Isaiah 53:5

You alone can heal me, you alone can save, and my praises are for you alone.
Jeremiah 17:14

The Benefit of Healing—II
The Moment She Touched Him, She Was Healed

The moment she did it, the flow of blood dried up. She could feel the change, and knew her plague was over and done with.

At the same moment, Jesus felt energy discharging from him. He turned around to the crowd and asked, "Who touched my robe?"

His disciples said, "What are you talking about? With this crowd pushing and jostling you, you're asking, 'Who touched me?' Dozens have touched you!"

But he went on asking, looking around to see who had done it.
—Mark 5:28–32

This woman was supernaturally healed. God is supernatural. He cannot be limited by what is natural because He created everything in the natural world. The only thing God is limited by is His character.

Throughout Scripture, we see God's healing touch on people's lives. This is who God is—our Healer. Yet, He doesn't always choose to heal us in supernatural ways. God created within our bodies healing properties. He also gives us wisdom in how to properly care for ourselves spiritually, emotionally, and physically.

So, when we ask God to heal us, the answer can come in many ways, but He is still the source. Be alert to His answer and don't limit Him.

The "Healing" Challenge

- Do you believe God desires to heal you?
- Has God been trying to speak to you about healing in some area of your life?
- Thank God for a specific time when He healed you naturally or supernaturally.

The "Healing" Declarations

Father, I will praise you and forget not all your benefits—you forgive all my sins and heal all my diseases.
Psalm 103:2–3

There is healing in your wings.
Malachi 4:2

The Benefit of Healing—III
Live Well, Live Blessed!

The woman, knowing what had happened, knowing she was the one, stepped up in fear and trembling, knelt before him, and gave him the whole story.

Jesus said to her, "Daughter, you took a risk of faith, and now you're healed and whole. Live well, live blessed! Be healed of your plague."

—Mark 5:33–34

Jesus was determined to confront the person who touched His robe. When the woman finally stepped forward, He made a link between her healing and her faith. He wanted to make sure she understood the role her faith played in her healing. Jesus could have let her go and just moved on, but this seemed important to Him.

So, it must be important for us to know, and that's why it is in His Word. When we step out in faith and believe that God will heal us, it's an invitation for Him to bring it on. Even though this woman was healed instantly, we might not be. Keep believing and asking, and never give up. Live well. Live blessed.

The "Healing" Challenge

- Have you given up on healing because it hasn't been instantaneous?
- What is the link between your faith and your healing?
- Memorize Hebrews 11:6.

The "Healing" Declarations

Father, I will pay attention to what you say; I will listen closely to your words. I will not let them out of my sight, I will keep them within my heart; for they are life and health to my whole body.
Proverbs 4:20–22

You heal my broken heart and bind up my wounds.
Psalm 147:3

The Benefit of Hope—I
She Had No Children

Each year Elkanah and his families journeyed to the Tabernacle at Shiloh to worship the Lord of the heavens and to sacrifice to him. (The priests on duty at that time were the two sons of Eli—Hophni and Phinehas.)

On the day he presented his sacrifice, Elkanah would celebrate the happy occasion by giving presents to Peninnah and her children; but although he loved Hannah very much, he could give her only one present, for the Lord had sealed her womb; so she had no children to give presents to. Peninnah made matters worse by taunting Hannah because of her barrenness. Every year it was the same—Peninnah scoffing and laughing at her as they went to Shiloh, making her cry so much she couldn't eat.

"What's the matter, Hannah?" Elkanah would exclaim. "Why aren't you eating? Why make such a fuss over having no children? Isn't having me better than having ten sons?"

—I Samuel 1:3–8 TLB

In Hannah's day, barrenness was a huge loss and an embarrassment to a family. That alone would have been difficult enough, but her husband's other wife teased Hannah to the point of tears. The situation appeared hopeless.

We all face difficulties that appear hopeless, and they would be without God. But with God there is always hope.

The "Hope" Challenge

- Are you facing a situation that appears hopeless?
- Where are you placing your hope?
- Lift up a situation that appears hopeless to the God who always offers hope.

The "Hope" Declarations

Father, your eyes are on me as I fear you, and I put my hope in your unfailing love.
                    Psalm 33:18

I will be strong and take heart, because my hope is in you.
                    Psalm 31:24

The Benefit of Hope—II
Give Me a Son

One evening after supper, when they were at Shiloh, Hannah went over to the Tabernacle. Eli the priest was sitting at his customary place beside the entrance. She was in deep anguish and was crying bitterly as she prayed to the Lord.

And she made this vow: "O Lord of heaven, if you will look down upon my sorrow and answer my prayer and give me a son, then I will give him back to you, and he'll be yours for his entire lifetime, and his hair shall never be cut."

—I Samuel 1:9–11 TLB

In the midst of her anguish, Hannah put her hope in the Lord, not in her husband and not in Eli the priest. Hope can be defined as *confident expectation*. But in difficult situations, it's natural to feel hopeless. Hopelessness is based on the here and now, and on what appears to be a no-win situation. But when we place our hope in God, we can confidently expect a good future.

No matter how bleak your situation may seem, you can confidently expect that God will make a way when there seems to be no way. Renew your hope in God. He won't disappoint you.

The "Hope" Challenge

- Do you tend to feel hopeless in difficult situations?
- Has God ever disappointed you?
- Meditate on God as the only One worthy of your confident expectation.

The "Hope" Declarations

Father, as I put my hope in you, you will renew my strength. I will soar on wings like eagles; I will run and not grow weary, I will walk and not be faint.

Isaiah 40:31

But as for me, I will always have hope; I will praise you more and more.

Psalm 71:14 NIV

The Benefit of Hope—III
Baby Samuel

Eli noticed her mouth moving as she was praying silently and, hearing no sound, thought she had been drinking.
"Must you come here drunk?" he demanded. "Throw away your bottle."
"Oh, no, sir!" she replied, "I'm not drunk! But I am very sad and I was pouring out my heart to the Lord. Please don't think that I am just some drunken bum!"
"In that case," Eli said, "cheer up! May the Lord of Israel grant you your petition, whatever it is!"
"Oh, thank you, sir!" she exclaimed, and went happily back, and began to take her meals again.
The entire family was up early the next morning and went to the Tabernacle to worship the Lord once more. Then they returned home to Ramah, and when Elkanah slept with Hannah, the Lord remembered her petition; in the process of time, a baby boy was born to her. She named him Samuel (meaning "asked of God") because, as she said, "I asked the Lord for him."
—I Samuel 1:12–20 TLB

God brought Hannah from the depths of despair to a place of radiant hope. He wants to do the same for you.

The "Hope" Challenge

▸ Do you feel that you pour your heart out to the Lord in vain?
▸ Do you need to renew your hope in the Lord?
▸▸ Radiate God's hope to someone in despair.

The "Hope" Declarations

Father, I do not lose heart. Though outwardly I am wasting away, yet inwardly I am being renewed day by day. For my light and momentary troubles are achieving for me an eternal glory that far outweighs them all.
2 Corinthians 4:16–18

I will hold unswervingly to the hope I profess, for you are faithful.
Hebrews 10:23–24

The Benefit of Humility—I
A Towel Around His Waist

Before the Passover celebration, Jesus knew that his hour had come to leave this world and return to his Father. He now showed the disciples the full extent of his love. It was time for supper, and the Devil had already enticed Judas, son of Simon Iscariot, to carry out his plan to betray Jesus.

Jesus knew that the Father had given him authority over everything and that he had come from God and would return to God. So he got up from the table, took off his robe, wrapped a towel around his waist, and poured water into a basin. Then he began to wash the disciples' feet and to wipe them with the towel he had around him.
—John 13:1–5 NLT

God had given Jesus authority over everything. Yet, here He prepared to wash feet. What an amazing picture! There wasn't a prideful bone in Jesus' body. He had a lowly beginning in a barn, His triumphal entry into Jerusalem was on a donkey, and now He was going to wash feet.

If someone could have demanded royal treatment, Jesus could have. If Jesus, Almighty God's Son, took on the nature of a servant—we should do likewise.

The "Humility" Challenge

- Is humility a negative character quality?
- In what ways do you struggle with pride?
- Ask God to give you the nature of a servant.

The "Humility" Declarations

Father, I know my attitude should be the kind that was shown me by Jesus Christ. He laid aside his mighty power and glory, and did not demand and cling to his rights. Instead he took on the nature of a servant.
Philippians 2:5–7

If I humble myself before you, you will lift me up.
James 4:10

The Benefit of Humility—II
Wash My Feet?

When [Jesus] came to Simon Peter, Peter said to him, "Lord, why are you going to wash my feet?"
Jesus replied, "You don't understand now why I am doing it; someday you will."
"No," Peter protested, "you will never wash my feet!"
Jesus replied, "But if I don't wash you, you won't belong to me."
Simon Peter exclaimed, "Then wash my hands and head as well, Lord, not just my feet!" Jesus replied, "A person who has bathed all over does not need to wash, except for the feet, to be entirely clean."
—John 13:6–10 NLT

If Jesus had clung to His rights as God's Son, we wouldn't have a prayer. Instead, He set aside all privilege and honor and stepped into our world.

Jesus then went on to live a selfless life rather than one of self-importance. He didn't have to prove anything to anyone, but through His humility, He made a way for everyone. Humility understands that without God, we would be nothing, we would have nothing, and we could do nothing of lasting value. Jesus understood.

The "Humility" Challenge

- Why is it hard to let Jesus wash us?
- Do you cling to your rights, or do you lay them down?
- Humbly serve someone in a practical way today.

The "Humility" Declarations

Father, you live in the place where contrite, humble spirits dwell; and you refresh the humble and give new courage to those with repentant hearts.
Isaiah 57:15

If I try to honor myself I will be humbled; and if I humble myself I will be honored.
Luke 14:11

The Benefit of Humility—III
I Have Given You an Example to Follow

After washing their feet, he put on his robe again and sat down and asked, "Do you understand what I was doing? You call me 'Teacher' and 'Lord,' and you are right, because it is true. And since I, the Lord and Teacher, have washed your feet, you ought to wash each other's feet. I have given you an example to follow. Do as I have done to you."

—John 13:12–15 NLT

Jesus resisted pride because it would have defeated His purpose for coming to die for our sins. And, even though we don't always see it, pride defeats God's purposes for us. Pride comes between God and us, and keeps us from experiencing His best.

Pride causes us to be self-seeking, to demand our own way, to never admit we're wrong, to withhold forgiveness, and to want all the credit.

Don't be deceived. Pride is not your friend—it is a roadblock to everything God tries to do in you. Follow Jesus' example and see how humility adds value to your life and to the lives of those around you.

The "Humility" Challenge

- How would pride have defeated Jesus' purpose for coming?
- Can you think of a time when pride has served you well?
- List three ways you've allowed pride to cheat you out of God's best.

The "Humility" Declarations

Father, as I humble myself under your mighty hand, in your good time you will lift me up.

1 Peter 5:6

As I humble myself before you, I will be given every blessing and shall have wonderful peace.

Psalm 37:11

The Benefit of Inheritance—I
You Are an Heir

What a God we have! And how fortunate we are to have him, this Father of our Master Jesus! Because Jesus was raised from the dead, we've been given a brand-new life and have everything to live for, including a future in heaven—and the future starts now! God is keeping careful watch over us and the future. The Day is coming when you'll have it all—life healed and whole.
—I Peter 1:3–5

A new covenant came into effect when Jesus died, a covenant not unlike a will that takes effect when someone dies. When we surrendered our lives to Christ, we became members of God's family.

Through this new relationship, we became heirs of an eternal inheritance and our names were written in the Book of Life. God also made all the precious promises that were reserved for His children available to us. We became His beneficiaries!

This inheritance is incorruptible and irrevocable. Your inheritance is a sure thing because God carefully keeps watch over it. Let's rejoice that we are in His will.

The "Inheritance" Challenge

- How do you feel knowing God made you His heir?
- Is your name written in the Book of Life?
- Don't waste another day. Your future in heaven starts now.

The "Inheritance" Declarations

Father, now that I am Christ's, I am a true descendant of Abraham, and all of God's promises to him belong to me.
Galatians 3:29

Since I am your child, you have made me also an heir.
Galatians 4:7

The Benefit of Inheritance—II
No More Evil

There shall be nothing in the city that is evil; for the throne of God and of the Lamb will be there, and his servants will worship him. And they shall see his face; and his name shall be written on their foreheads. And there will be no night there—no need for lamps or sun—for the Lord God will be their light; and they shall reign forever and ever.
—Revelation 22:3–5 TLB

Heaven will be completely free of evil. Just imagine a city without evil. It's difficult to do, because evil is all we've ever known. We experience God's goodness in our short life span on earth, but we must continually battle evil.

This new heavenly city will be wonderful because we'll no longer hear terrible news reports. We won't be plagued by temptations—there will be no wrong choices to make. We won't need to ask forgiveness for anything, because sin will not be a part of heaven. There will be no darkness, just God's marvelous light. And nothing will keep us from His light and His presence ever again.

The "Inheritance" Challenge

- What might a city without evil be like?
- Do you look forward to worshiping God in heaven?
- Just imagine heaven.

The "Inheritance" Declarations

Father, you have assigned me my portion and my cup; you have made my lot secure. The boundary lines have fallen for me in pleasant places; surely I have a delightful inheritance.
Psalm 16:5–6

I have the Holy Spirit, who is a deposit guaranteeing my inheritance.
Ephesians 1:13–14

The Benefit of Inheritance—III
I Am Making Everything New!

"Now the dwelling of God is with men, and he will live with them. They will be his people, and God himself will be with them and be their God. He will wipe every tear from their eyes. There will be no more death or mourning or crying or pain, for the old order of things has passed away."

He who was seated on the throne said, "I am making everything new!"

—Revelation 21:3–5 NIV

When Jesus left Earth to return to heaven, He said He was going to prepare a place for us and that He would come back for us. What a day that will be, when we finally see our Lord face to face.

God's dwelling place is our final destination—the place we were meant to be. We'll never be completely at home in this world because we are just passing through. When we're finally with God, there will be no more death, no more saying goodbye to people we love. There will be no more sickness or crying or pain. God is making everything new.

The "Inheritance" Challenge

- Are you excited for Jesus' return, or do you dread it?
- Do you ever feel as if you're a stranger in a foreign land?
- Think about how you'll react when you see Jesus' face.

The "Inheritance" Declarations

Father, in love you predestined me to be adopted as your child through Jesus Christ, in accordance with your pleasure and will.
Ephesians 1:4–5

You have gone to prepare a place for me. And you will come back for me.
John 14:1–3

The Benefit of Joy—I
Jesus Called Him by Name

As Jesus was passing through Jericho, a man named Zacchaeus, one of the most influential Jews in the Roman tax–collecting business (and, of course, a very rich man), tried to get a look at Jesus, but he was too short to see over the crowds. So he ran ahead and climbed into a sycamore tree beside the road, to watch from there.

When Jesus came by he looked up at Zacchaeus and called him by name! "Zacchaeus!" he said. "Quick! Come down! For I am going to be a guest in your home today!"

—Luke 19:1–5 TLB

Zacchaeus just *had* to get a glimpse of Jesus. In fact, his desperation drove him to climb a tree to see Jesus.

Even though he ran a lucrative tax-collecting business and had prospered greatly from it, Zacchaeus was still searching. He knew something was missing in his life.

And then, the most amazing thing that can happen in the course of someone's life happened to Zacchaeus: Jesus called him by name. The most important guest Zacchaeus could ever have was about to come to his home.

Jesus knows you and calls you by name. When you invite Him in, He brings joy in all of its fullness with Him.

The "Joy" Challenge

- Where are the places you try to find joy?
- How often do you experience the fullness of joy?
- Reflect on how you felt when Jesus called you by name.

The "Joy" Declarations

Father, in your presence is fullness of joy; at your right hand are pleasures forevermore.

Psalm 16:11

You have filled my heart with greater joy than when their grain and new wine abound.

Psalm 4:7 NIV

The Benefit of Joy—II
Great Excitement and Joy

Zacchaeus hurriedly climbed down and took Jesus to his house in great excitement and joy. But the crowds were displeased. "He has gone to be the guest of a notorious sinner," they grumbled.
—Luke 19:6–7 TLB

Zacchaeus did not have a good reputation—he would not win any popularity contests. He was Jewish, but he collected taxes for the Roman government. The words *tax collector* in Jesus' time were synonymous with *crook* or *traitor*.

Paying taxes to such an ungodly government angered the Jewish people. Being gouged by the collectors also upset them. That's why the crowds grumbled over Jesus being Zacchaeus' houseguest.

Can you picture Zacchaeus scurrying down the tree? He probably thought himself unworthy of having Jesus as his guest. Yet, Jesus wanted to come. So, Zacchaeus took Jesus in with great excitement and joy. The crowd's displeasure could not take away his joy.

The world did not give us our joy and the world cannot take it away.

The "Joy" Challenge

▸ Do you often get excited about Jesus being in your life?
▸ Is there anything that can take your joy away?
▸▸ Hold on to God's joy throughout this day.

The "Joy" Declarations

Father, I will rejoice in you, I will be joyful in God my Savior.
Habakkuk 3:18

You have done so much for me, O Lord. No wonder I am glad! I sing for joy.
Psalm 92:4 TLB

The Benefit of Joy—III
The Joy of His Salvation

Meanwhile, Zacchaeus stood before the Lord and said, "Sir, from now on I will give half my wealth to the poor, and if I find I have overcharged anyone on his taxes, I will penalize myself by giving him back four times as much!"

Jesus told him, "This shows that salvation has come to this home today. This man was one of the lost sons of Abraham, and I, the Messiah, have come to search for and to save such souls as his."
—Luke 19:8–9 TLB

Zacchaeus had a smile on the inside he'd never experienced before and a new bounce in his step. He'd been a lost soul, now he was found—and it showed in his actions.

Nothing compares to the joy that comes with salvation. Jesus is the only source of joy. Oh, some things in this world can make us high and give us pleasure, but that happiness is fleeting.

Happiness is a feeling that comes from good or fun happenings. But the joy that Jesus brings is deep, everlasting, and it doesn't depend on happenings.

Continually live in the joy of your salvation and you will be contagious.

The "Joy" Challenge

- Do you continually remember and experience the joy of your salvation?
- Are you a pleasure-seeking person who looks to circumstances for joy?
- Help someone discover God's joy today.

The "Joy" Declarations

Father, restore to me the joy of your salvation and grant me a willing spirit, to sustain me.
Psalm 51:12

This is the day you have made; I will rejoice and be glad in it.
Psalm 118:24

The Benefit of a New Heart—I
Paul Tried to Destroy the Church

Do you think I [Paul] speak this strongly in order to manipulate crowds? Or curry favor with God? Or get popular applause? If my goal was popularity, I wouldn't bother being Christ's slave.

Know this—I am most emphatic here, friends—this great Message I delivered to you is not mere human optimism. I didn't receive it through the traditions, and I wasn't taught it in some school. I got it straight from God, received the Message directly from Jesus Christ.

I'm sure that you've heard the story of my earlier life when I lived in the Jewish way. In those days I went all out in persecuting God's church. I was systematically destroying it.
—Galatians 1:10–14

Sometimes the hardest people to reach with the Good News are those who are outwardly religious, like Paul. While he enthusiastically and sincerely kept the Jewish law, he was obsessed with destroying Christians. Paul, like all of us, desperately needed to be changed inwardly—he needed a heart transplant.

Without God, our hearts are hopelessly dark and deceitful. With God, we can have a heart that beats with His.

The "New Heart" Challenge

- Looking back, do you see how dark your heart was before God changed it?
- Can being outwardly religious bring inward changes?
- Reflect on the changes in your life since God gave you a new heart.

The "New Heart" Declarations

Father, you have given me a new heart, new and right desires, and put a new Spirit within me. You have taken away my stony heart of sin and given me a new heart of love.
Ezekiel 36:26

I have chosen the way of truth; I have set my heart on your laws.
Psalm 119:30 NIV

The Benefit of a New Heart—II
Paul Had a Change of Heart

I was so enthusiastic about the traditions of my ancestors that I advanced head and shoulders above my peers in my career. Even then God had designs on me. Why, when I was still in my mother's womb he chose and called me out of sheer generosity! Now he has intervened and revealed his Son to me so that I might joyfully tell non–Jews about him.
—Galatians 1:15–16

God intervened in Paul's life. Paul was enthusiastic about his desires, but his desires were dead wrong. God wanted to give Paul the right desires and the right thoughts that would result in the right choices.

God wants to do the same for you. He gives you a fresh start in life—a clean slate. God wants to continually transform your thoughts and give you the right desires so that your old desires will die.

With God, your old way of life ends and a new life begins—you are a new creation.

The "New Heart" Challenge

- What are some behaviors you've failed to correct on your own?
- How do you feel knowing that you are a new creation?
- Consider the ways God has transformed your thoughts and desires.

The "New Heart" Declarations

Father, as a Christian I have no veil over my face; I can be a mirror that brightly reflects your glory. And as your Spirit works within me, I become more and more like you.
2 Corinthians 3:18

Because I am in Christ, I am a new creation; the old has gone, the new has come!
2 Corinthians 5:17

The Benefit of a New Heart—III
A New Life Begins

Then I began my ministry in the regions of Syria and Cilicia. After all that time and activity I was still unknown by face among the Christian churches in Judea. There was only this report: "That man who once persecuted us is now preaching the very message he used to try to destroy." Their response was to recognize and worship God because of me!
—Galatians 1:21–24

When God got hold of Paul, he had an about-face. He enthusiastically began building up the church he previously tried to destroy. People were amazed that the man who once vehemently persecuted them now preached to them. Because of Paul's transformation, people recognized God at work in his life and they worshipped Him for it.

When we are in Christ, we can no longer say, "I'll never change!" If God was able to change a heart like Paul's, He can change any heart. And the world will take notice.

The "New Heart" Challenge

- Would the changes that people see in you cause them to worship God?
- How often do you use the excuse, "That's just the way I am!"
- Tell someone today how God has changed your life.

The "New Heart" Declarations

Father, instead of becoming so well-adjusted to my culture so that I fit into it without even thinking, I will fix my attention on you and be transformed from the inside out.
Romans 12:2

You began at the very center of who I was and are working from the center outward, cleaning up my life as I trust and believe in you.
Acts 15:9

The Benefit of Perseverance—I
The Long Shipbuilding Project

As God observed how bad it was, and saw that all mankind was vicious and depraved, he said to Noah, "I have decided to destroy all mankind; for the earth is filled with crime because of man. Yes, I will destroy mankind from the earth.

"Make a boat from resinous wood, sealing it with tar; and construct decks and stalls throughout the ship. Make it 450 feet long, 75 feet wide, and 45 feet high. Construct a skylight all the way around the ship, eighteen inches below the roof; and make three decks inside the boat—a bottom, middle, and upper deck—and put a door in the side.

"Look! I am going to cover the earth with a flood and destroy every living being—everything in which there is the breath of life. All will die.

"But I promise to keep you safe in the ship, with your wife and your sons and their wives."
—Genesis 6:12–18 TLB

Noah had a huge project in front of him. I believe the one thing that gave Noah the staying power during this project was God's promise: God said He would keep Noah and his family safe—and Noah believed Him. Depend on His promises.

The "Perseverance" Challenge

- Do you easily see things through to the finish?
- What frustrates you about long-term projects?
- Memorize a promise in God's Word, and depend on it.

The "Perseverance" Declarations

Father, I will not get tired of doing what is right, for after a while I will reap a harvest of blessing if I don't get discouraged and give up.
Galatians 6:9

You will fill me with your mighty, glorious strength so that I can keep going no matter what happens.
Colossians 1:11

The Benefit of Perseverance—II
The Long Ride

God didn't forget about Noah and all the animals in the boat! He sent a wind to blow across the waters, and the floods began to disappear, for the subterranean water sources ceased their gushing, and the torrential rains subsided.

So the flood gradually receded until, 150 days after it began, the boat came to rest upon the mountains of Ararat. Three months later, as the waters continued to go down, other mountain peaks appeared.
—Genesis 8:1–5 TLB

I'm sure that while Noah was building this big boat, he and his family endured ridicule. Then, when the flood finally came, Noah spent many months living on the boat—and this was no cruise! There was no midnight buffet, and Noah's family really did live in a zoo.

God didn't forget about Noah, and He hasn't forgotten about you. He will help you to be steadfast so you can endure the long and challenging ride.

The "Perseverance" Challenge

- Do you depend on God to give the endurance you need?
- Have you ever felt that God has forgotten about you?
- Consider how difficult times in your life have helped you develop patience.

The "Perseverance" Declarations

Father, I can rejoice when I run into problems and trials, for I know that they are good for me—they help me learn to be patient. And patience develops strength of character in me and helps me trust you more each time I use it until finally my hope and faith are strong and steady.
Romans 5:3–4

I've got my eye on the goal, where you are beckoning me onward—to Jesus. I'm off and running, and I'm not turning back.
Philippians 3:14

The Benefit of Perseverance—III
The Destination

Then Noah built an altar and sacrificed on it some of the animals and birds God had designated for that purpose. And Jehovah was pleased with the sacrifice and said to himself, "I will never do it again—I will never again curse the earth, destroying all living things, even though man's bent is always toward evil from his earliest youth, and even though he does such wicked things. As long as the earth remains, there will be springtime and harvest, cold and heat, winter and summer, day and night."
—Genesis 8:20–22 TLB

Noah stayed the course through faith and got everything God had promised to him. And the altar Noah built would help him and future generations remember God's faithfulness to get them through.

The "Perseverance" Challenge

- Do you often reflect on the faithfulness of God that has gotten you through?
- How does remembering God's faithfulness help you in life now?
- Encourage someone today by reminding them of God's faithfulness.

The "Perseverance" Declarations

Father, I will throw off everything that hinders me and the sin that so easily entangles, and I will run with perseverance the race marked out for me. I will fix my eyes on Jesus, the author and perfecter of my faith, who for the joy set before him endured the cross, scorning its shame, and sat down at your right hand. I will consider him who endured such opposition from sinful men, so that I will not grow weary and lose heart.
Hebrews 12:1–3

I will pursue righteousness, godliness, faith, love, perseverance and gentleness. I will fight the good fight of faith, and take hold of the eternal life to which I was called.
1 Timothy 6:11–12

The Benefit of Personal Growth—I
Nursing Babes

But for right now, friends, I'm completely frustrated by your unspiritual dealings with each other and with God. You're acting like infants in relation to Christ, capable of nothing much more than nursing at the breast. Well, then, I'll nurse you since you don't seem capable of anything more. As long as you grab for what makes you feel good or makes you look important, are you really much different than a babe at the breast, content only when everything's going your way?
—1 Corinthians 3:1–3

These Christians frustrated Paul because they acted like babies. They, like babies, were happy as long as everything went well in their little world. But this attitude stopped them from growing in Christ. Paul expected them to be more mature at this point.

Just as healthy babies are expected to grow up, we are expected to grow up in Christ. Let's stop nursing and grow up!

The "Personal Growth" Challenge

- What in your life is stunting your growth in Christ?
- Are there ways you're still baby-like spiritually?
- Ask God to give you a desire to mature in Christ.

The "Personal Growth" Declarations

Father, you want me to grow up, to know the whole truth and tell it in love—like Christ in everything. I take my lead from Christ, who is the source of everything I do. He keeps me in step with others. His very breath and blood flow through me, nourishing me so that I will grow up healthy in you, robust in love.
Ephesians 4:15–16

I long to grow up into the fullness of your salvation.
1 Peter 2:2

The Benefit of Personal Growth—II
God Makes You Grow

When one of you says, "I'm on Paul's side," and another says, "I'm for Apollos," aren't you being totally infantile?
Who do you think Paul is, anyway? Or Apollos, for that matter? Servants, both of us—servants who waited on you as you gradually learned to entrust your lives to our mutual Master. We each carried out our servant assignment. I planted the seed, Apollos watered the plants, but God made you grow.
—1 Corinthians 3:4–6

Just as a runner in training will never improve by merely watching other runners run, Christians cannot mature without experiencing Christ personally.

We can't just learn about prayer, we have to pray. We can't just hear God's Word from the pulpit, we have to meditate on it and practice it ourselves. And we can't just be pew warmers, we have to minister to those around us.

Prayer, God's Word, and ministry are Miracle Grow in God's hands.

The "Personal Growth" Challenge

▸ Does your dependence on others keep your faith from growing?
▸ How much time do you spend putting God's Word in your heart?
▸▸ Create a personal growth plan for prayer, Bible study, and ministry.

The "Personal Growth" Declarations

Father, I will flourish like a palm tree and grow tall as the cedars of Lebanon. For I am transplanted into your own garden and am under your personal care. Even in old age I will still produce fruit and be vital and green.
Psalm 92:12–15

I will consider it pure joy, whenever I face trials of many kinds, because I know that the testing of my faith develops perseverance. Perseverance must finish its work so that I may be mature and complete, not lacking anything.
James 1:2–4

The Benefit of Personal Growth—III
Gardening Tools

It's not the one who plants or the one who waters who is at the center of this process but God, who makes things grow. Planting and watering are menial servant jobs at minimum wages. What makes them worth doing is the God we are serving. You happen to be God's field in which we are working.
—1 Corinthians 3:7–9

God uses other godly servants to help us mature in Christ. These people are grounded in God's Word, are following Christ's example, are mature, and can nurture us in our faith. If you don't have these nurturing people in your life, you should recruit some.

In turn, as we mature in Christ, God expects us to do the same for others: to pass to them what we've learned and gained through our Christian experience. We need to be the servants God uses to help others grow. As long as you live in Christ, you ought to grow in Christ and help others do the same.

The "Personal Growth" Challenge

- Who in your life nurtures you in your faith?
- In what ways are you experiencing personal growth now?
- Help someone today to grow in Christ.

The "Personal Growth" Declarations

Father, I will be able to eat solid spiritual food and understand the deeper things of your Word when I learn right from wrong by practicing doing right.
Hebrews 5:14

I will let my roots grow down into you and draw up nourishment from you. I will go on growing in you, and become strong and vigorous in the truth I was taught.
Colossians 2:7

The Benefit of Praise—I
Jehoshaphat's Prayer

"O Lord God of our fathers—the only God in all the heavens, the Ruler of all the kingdoms of the earth—you are so powerful, so mighty. Who can stand against you? O our God, didn't you drive out the heathen who lived in this land when your people arrived? And didn't you give this land forever to the descendants of your friend Abraham?

"Your people settled here and built this Temple for you, truly believing that in a time like this—whenever we are faced with any calamity such as war, disease, or famine—we can stand here before this Temple and before you—for you are here in this Temple—and cry out to you to save us; and that you will hear us and rescue us."
—2 Chronicles 20:6–9 TLB

Jehoshaphat was badly shaken by the news that a vast army was marching against him. He knew the people of Judah had no way to protect themselves against this mighty army. Jehoshaphat didn't know what to do—so He turned to God.

He started by acknowledging who God is and how powerful He is. In other words, Jehoshaphat began to praise. Praise helped him and the people of Judah gain the proper perspective.

The "Praise" Challenge

- How does praising God help you gain perspective?
- How could your knowledge of God help you to praise Him?
- Make praise a part of every prayer.

The "Praise" Declarations

Father, how lovely is your dwelling place! My soul yearns, even faints for you; my heart and my flesh cry out for you, the living God.
Psalm 84:1–2

Among the gods there is none like you, no deeds can compare with yours.
Psalm 86:8 NIV

The Benefit of Praise—II
Praise Songs

"Listen to me, all you people of Judah and Jerusalem, and you, O king Jehoshaphat!" he exclaimed. "The Lord says, 'Don't be afraid! Don't be paralyzed by this mighty army! For the battle is not yours, but God's!

"'Tomorrow, go down and attack them! You will find them coming up the slopes of Ziz at the end of the valley that opens into the wilderness of Jeruel. But you will not need to fight! Take your places; stand quietly and see the incredible rescue operation God will perform for you, O people of Judah and Jerusalem! Don't be afraid or discouraged! Go out there tomorrow, for the Lord is with you!'"

Then King Jehoshaphat fell to the ground with his face to the earth, and all the people of Judah and the people of Jerusalem did the same, worshiping the Lord. Then the Levites of the Kohath clan and the Korah clan stood to praise the Lord God of Israel with songs of praise that rang out strong and clear.
—2 Chronicles 20:15–19 TLB

Jehoshaphat's praise-filled prayer created an atmosphere where God's Spirit could move, and it placed everyone in a posture of attentiveness to God. That's when Judah heard from God, and the praise continued.

The "Praise" Challenge

- Have you sensed God's presence in your praises?
- Do you praise God in the midst of a crisis?
- Focus your attention on God as you read aloud Psalm 113.

The "Praise" Declarations

Father, your love reaches to the heavens, your faithfulness to the skies. Your righteousness is like the mighty mountains, your justice like the great deep.
Psalm 36:5–6

I will praise you with all my heart; I will tell of all your wonders.
Psalm 9:1

The Benefit of Praise—III
Garments of Praise

Early the next morning the army of Judah went out into the wilderness of Tekoa. On the way Jehoshaphat stopped and called them to attention. "Listen to me, O people of Judah and Jerusalem," he said. "Believe in the Lord your God and you shall have success! Believe his prophets, and everything will be all right!"

After consultation with the leaders of the people, he determined that there should be a choir leading the march, clothed in sanctified garments and singing the song "His Lovingkindness Is Forever" as they walked along praising and thanking the Lord!

And at the moment they began to sing and to praise, the Lord caused the armies of Ammon, Moab, and Mount Seir to begin fighting among themselves, and they destroyed each other!
—2 Chronicles 20:20–22 TLB

While the choir led Judah's army in singing praises, God worked out their victory. This account of Jehoshaphat began with a spirit of heavyheartedness, but quickly changed to a spirit of praise. A happy ending was written with songs of praise.

We should continually offer sacrifices of praise to God, even when we're heavyhearted. He is always worthy, and we will always benefit from it.

The "Praise" Challenge

▸ How might praise help when you're heavyhearted?
▸ Why would God choose to bring victory in the context of praise?
▸▸ Memorize a praise song to sing when you're heavyhearted.

The "Praise" Declarations

Father, I will glorify your name forever. For great is your love toward me; you have delivered me from the depths of the grave.
Psalm 86:12–13

I will bless you at all times; your praise shall continually be in my mouth.
Psalm 34:1

The Benefit of Prayer—I
The Church Prayed

All the time that Peter was under heavy guard in the jailhouse, the church prayed for him most strenuously.
Then the time came for Herod to bring him out for the kill. That night, even though shackled to two soldiers, one on either side, Peter slept like a baby. And there were guards at the door keeping their eyes on the place. Herod was taking no chances!
Suddenly there was an angel at his side and light flooding the room. The angel shook Peter and got him up: "Hurry!" The handcuffs fell off his wrists. The angel said, "Get dressed. Put on your shoes." Peter did it. Then, "Grab your coat and let's get out of here." Peter followed him, but didn't believe it was really an angel—he thought he was dreaming.
—Acts 12:5–9

The church interceded in prayer for Peter because they believed prayer would significantly affect Peter's outcome. Even though things looked bleak for Peter in the natural world, things in the supernatural world were moving and shaking.

God worked through the prayers of His church then, and He still works today. God wants to powerfully influence someone's world through your prayers—even your own.

The "Prayer" Challenge

▸ Why would God choose to work through the prayers of His people?
▸ Do you believe that your prayers have a powerful impact?
▸▸ Strenuously pray for someone needing God's influence.

The "Prayer" Declarations

Father, I can approach your throne of grace with confidence, so that I may receive mercy and find grace to help me in my time of need.
Hebrews 4:16

I thank you that my prayers are powerful and effective.
James 5:16

The Benefit of Prayer—II
Rhoda Forgot to Open the Door

Past the first guard and then the second, they came to the iron gate that led into the city. It swung open before them on its own, and they were out on the street, free as the breeze. At the first intersection the angel left him, going his own way. That's when Peter realized it was no dream. "I can't believe it—this really happened! The Master sent his angel and rescued me from Herod's vicious little production and the spectacle the Jewish mob was looking forward to."

Still shaking his head, amazed, he went to Mary's house, the Mary who was John Mark's mother. The house was packed with praying friends. When he knocked on the door to the courtyard, a young woman named Rhoda came to see who it was. But when she recognized his voice—Peter's voice!—she was so excited and eager to tell everyone Peter was there that she forgot to open the door and left him standing in the street.

—Acts 12:10–14

While Peter's friends were still praying, God provided the answer to their prayer. Now that's the kind of fast response time we like these days!

We can always be sure that God will answer our prayers, but we won't know how or when.

The "Prayer" Challenge

▸ Do you wait expectantly, knowing God will answer your prayers?
▸ How can you know that God always answers prayers?
▸▸ Thank God for a specific prayer He's answered.

The "Prayer" Declarations

Father, in the morning you hear my voice; in the morning I lay my requests before you and wait in expectation.

Psalm 5:3

I call on you for you will answer me.

Psalm 17:6

The Benefit of Prayer—III
They Didn't Recognize the Answer

But they wouldn't believe her, dismissing her, dismissing her report. "You're crazy," they said. She stuck by her story, insisting. They still wouldn't believe her and said, "It must be his angel." All this time poor Peter was standing out in the street, knocking away.

Finally they opened up and saw him—and went wild! Peter put his hands up and calmed them down. He described how the Master had gotten him out of jail, then said, "Tell James and the brothers what's happened." He left them and went off to another place.
—Acts 12:15–17

Because God answered Peter's friends' prayer with a miraculous deliverance, we can make some safe assumptions: their request aligned with God's character and desire, they had the right motives, they prayed earnestly. There were no hindrances keeping God from granting their request.

They seemed to do everything right except one thing—they didn't recognize the answer when it came. When we make our request to God and expectantly wait for His answer, we also need to watch for the answer.

The "Prayer" Challenge

- Why do our requests to God need to align with His character?
- How often do you watch for God's answer to your prayers?
- Ask God to help you recognize His answers to prayer.

The "Prayer" Declarations

Father, if I ask it will be given to me; If I seek I will find; If I knock the door will be opened to me.
Matthew 7:7–8

You answer me with awesome deeds of righteousness.
Psalm 65:5

The Benefit of Prosperity—I
Jehovah's Blessings

Soon after the birth of Joseph to Rachel, Jacob said to Laban, "I want to go back home. Let me take my wives and children—for I earned them from you—and be gone, for you know how fully I have paid for them with my service to you."

"Please don't leave me," Laban replied, "for a fortune-teller that I consulted told me that the many blessings I've been enjoying are all because of your being here. How much of a raise do you need to get you to stay? Whatever it is, I'll pay it."

Jacob replied, "You know how faithfully I've served you through these many years, and how your flocks and herds have grown. For it was little indeed you had before I came, and your wealth has increased enormously; Jehovah has blessed you from everything I do! But now, what about me? When should I provide for my own family?"
—Genesis 30:25–30 TLB

God wants to make us rich in every way so we can help further the gospel, provide for our families, and generously meet the needs of others. God doesn't want to give us increase for our benefit alone. We are blessed to be a blessing.

The "Prosperity" Challenge

- Would God ever choose to impoverish His children?
- In what ways have you been blessed to be a blessing?
- Give generously to someone in need.

The "Prosperity" Declarations

Father, I will be made rich in every way so that I can be generous on every occasion. And through me, your generosity will result in thanksgiving to you.
2 Corinthians 9:11

You find pleasure in the prosperity of your servant.
Psalm 35:27

The Benefit of Prosperity—II
Streaked and Spotted Lambs and Kids

Then Jacob took fresh shoots from poplar, almond, and plane trees, and peeled white streaks in them, and placed these rods beside the watering troughs so that the flocks would see them when they came to drink; for that is when they mated. So the flocks mated before the white-streaked rods, and their offspring were streaked and spotted, and Jacob added them to his flock.

Then he divided out the ewes from Laban's flock and segregated them from the rams, and let them mate only with Jacob's black rams. Thus he built his flocks from Laban's.

Moreover, he watched for the stronger animals to mate, and placed the peeled branches before them, but didn't with the feebler ones. So the less healthy lambs were Laban's and the stronger ones were Jacob's! As a result, Jacob's flocks increased rapidly and he became very wealthy, with many servants, camels, and donkeys.
—Genesis 30:37–43 TLB

God helped Jacob come up with a brilliant business plan. Then He prospered Jacob in his career as a herdsman. God made it possible for Jacob to go from a poor servant to a rich livestock owner.

As you delight in doing what God wants, you will prosper.

The "Prosperity" Challenge

- Has God prospered you in your career?
- What is your attitude about wealth?
- Ask God to give you a godly attitude about wealth.

The "Prosperity" Declarations

Father, I delight in doing everything you want me to, I will be like a tree along a riverbank bearing luscious fruit each season without fail. My leaves shall never wither, and all I do shall prosper.
Psalm 1:2–3

As I am diligent, my plans will surely lead to abundance.
Proverbs 21:5

The Benefit of Prosperity—III
God Made Me Wealthy

So one day Jacob sent for Rachel and Leah to come out to the field where he was with the flocks, to talk things over with them.

"Your father has turned against me," he told them, "and now the God of my fathers has come and spoken to me. You know how hard I've worked for your father, but he has been completely unscrupulous and has broken his wage contract with me again and again and again.

"But God has not permitted him to do me any harm! For if he said the speckled animals would be mine, then all the flock produced speckled; and when he changed and said I could have the streaked ones, then all the lambs were streaked! In this way God has made me wealthy at your father's expense."

—Genesis 31:4–9 TLB

No matter how Laban tried to take advantage of Jacob, God wouldn't let Laban harm him. God can do whatever He wants with His wealth, and it pleases Him to prosper His children with it.

The "Prosperity" Challenge

- When people take advantage of you, can God still prosper you?
- Are you sowing seeds of hard work and honesty so God can prosper you?
- Faithfully give back to God a portion of what He's faithfully given to you.

The "Prosperity" Declarations

Father, as I bring the whole tithe into the storehouse, there will be food in my house. And you will throw open the floodgates of heaven and pour out so much blessing that I will not have room enough for it.

Malachi 3:10–11

I thank you that in all respects I will prosper and be in good health, just as my soul prospers.

3 John 2–3

The Benefit of Reconciliation—I
Payback Time

Then Joseph returned to Egypt with his brothers and all who had accompanied him to the funeral of his father. But now that their father was dead, Joseph's brothers were frightened.
"Now Joseph will pay us back for all the evil we did to him," they said.
—Genesis 50:14–16 TLB

Joseph was Jacob's favorite son, which was so obvious to Joseph's brothers they decided to get rid of him. They sold him to slave traders traveling to Egypt, and then told Jacob a ferocious animal had killed Joseph.

Potiphar, one of Pharaoh's officials in Egypt, bought Joseph and put him in charge of his household. But when Potiphar's wife falsely accused Joseph of a crime, he was thrown into jail for two years.

One day, Pharaoh had a dream, and God gave Joseph the ability to interpret the dream. Grateful, Pharaoh not only released Joseph from jail, he also made him second-in-command.

When a famine struck the land, Jacob and his sons came to Egypt to get food and Joseph offered them a place to live. At Jacob's death, Joseph's brothers feared it was payback time.

But God worked all things together for the good of everyone, and He had a much better plan for their family—reconciliation.

The "Reconciliation" Challenge

▸ Which relationships in your life need reconciliation right now?
▸ Do you believe that God desires to reconcile broken relationships?
▸▸ Show love to someone who has hurt you.

The "Reconciliation" Declarations

Father, you are my peace, and you came to destroy the barriers and walls that divide.
You want us to be reconciled to you and to each other.
Ephesians 2:14–16

A cord of three strands is not quickly broken.
Ecclesiastes 4:12b NIV

The Benefit of Reconciliation—II
Forgive Us

So they sent him this message: "Before he died, your father instructed us to tell you to forgive us for the great evil we did to you. We servants of the God of your father beg you to forgive us." When Joseph read the message, he broke down and cried.
Then his brothers came and fell down before him and said, "We are your slaves."
—Genesis 50:17–18 TLB

On one end of this relationship chasm is Joseph, who was completely rejected by his brothers. On the other end are Joseph's brothers because they completely betrayed Joseph.

From a human perspective, it seemed impossible for them to patch things up. But with God, all things are possible, and relationships are extremely important to Him.

God first wants our relationship with Him to be reconciled and then our relationship with others. And because you have been reconciled to God, you can now be a minister of reconciliation.

The "Reconciliation" Challenge

▸ Why are relationships so important to God?
▸ Are there ever relationships that are impossible to reconcile?
▸▸ Ask God to use you as a minister of reconciliation.

The "Reconciliation" Declarations

Father, you reconciled me to yourself through Christ and gave me the ministry of reconciliation; you reconciled the world to yourself in Christ, not counting men's sins against them. And you have committed to me the message of reconciliation. I am therefore Christ's ambassador, as though God were making his appeal through me. You made him who had no sin to be sin for me, so that in him I might become the righteousness of God.
2 Corinthians 5:18–21

I will not separate what you have joined together.
Matthew 19:6

The Benefit of Reconciliation—III
Am I God?

But Joseph told them, "Don't be afraid of me. Am I God, to judge and punish you? As far as I am concerned, God turned into good what you meant for evil, for he brought me to this high position I have today so that I could save the lives of many people. No, don't be afraid. Indeed, I myself will take care of you and your families."
And he spoke very kindly to them, reassuring them.
—Genesis 50:19–21 TLB

Forgiveness is the heart of reconciliation. Because God forgave us, our relationship with Him can be reestablished. God forgave us, not because we deserved it, but because He loves us.

We, like Joseph, have been wronged and hurt by people, and we need to forgive as Joseph forgave. Not only did Joseph forgive his brothers, he also said he would take care of them, he spoke kindly to them, and he reassured them.

As far as it concerns you, do everything you can to reestablish relationships in your life. And, offer forgiveness in word and action.

The "Reconciliation" Challenge

- Do you forgive others as Christ forgave you?
- Do you show forgiveness in your words and in your actions?
- Forgive someone.

The "Reconciliation" Declarations

Father, if I am offering my gift at the altar and there remember that my brother has something against me, I will leave my gift there in front of the altar. First I will go and be reconciled to my brother, then I'll come and offer my gift.
Matthew 5:23–24

In you, old waste places will be built up; the foundations of many generations will be raised up; and breaches will be repaired.
Isaiah 58:12

The Benefit of Resisting Temptation—I
Joseph Has Great Success

The Lord was with Joseph and blessed him greatly as he served in the home of his Egyptian master. Potiphar noticed this and realized that the Lord was with Joseph, giving him success in everything he did. So Joseph naturally became quite a favorite with him.

Potiphar soon put Joseph in charge of his entire household and entrusted him with all his business dealings. From the day Joseph was put in charge, the Lord began to bless Potiphar for Joseph's sake. All his household affairs began to run smoothly, and his crops and livestock flourished. So Potiphar gave Joseph complete administrative responsibility over everything he owned.

With Joseph there, he didn't have a worry in the world, except to decide what he wanted to eat!

—Genesis 39:2–6 NLT

At seventeen, Joseph was arrogant and spoiled. So, his brothers sold him into slavery. A rich Egyptian official bought him. The Lord gave Joseph success in everything he did, and he had control over everything in the official's house.

Joseph could have boasted about his success and new status. But I think his past experience with arrogance helped him resist the temptation.

The "Resisting Temptation" Challenge

- How can past sins help us to resist similar temptations now?
- Where do you think temptation comes from?
- Tell a friend about a temptation you're struggling with.

The "Resisting Temptation" Declarations

Father, I will watch and pray so that I will not fall into temptation. My spirit is willing, but my body is weak.
Matthew 26:41

Since Christ himself has now been through suffering and temptation, he knows what it is like when I suffer and am tempted, and he is wonderfully able to help me.
Hebrews 2:18

The Benefit of Resisting Temptation—II
A Great Sin Against God

Now Joseph was a very handsome and well-built young man. And about this time, Potiphar's wife began to desire him and invited him to sleep with her. But Joseph refused. "Look," he told her, "my master trusts me with everything in his entire household. No one here has more authority than I do! He has held back nothing from me except you, because you are his wife. How could I ever do such a wicked thing? It would be a great sin against God."
—Genesis 39:6–9 NLT

While Potiphar's wife gave in to her lustful desires, Joseph resisted. They both made a choice. Joseph didn't want to betray his master's trust. More importantly, he knew that giving in would be a great sin against God.

Even though sin looks deceitfully appealing, it always leads to the destruction of many lives, and eventually death. It isn't a sin to be tempted—giving in is.

The "Resisting Temptation" Challenge

- Have you ever thought that God tested you by tempting you to sin?
- Do you realize that when you give in to temptation, you are offending God?
- Consider how your actions may cause temptation for someone else.

The "Resisting Temptation" Declarations

Father, I will remember, when I want to do wrong it is never you tempting me, for you never want to do wrong and never tempt anyone else to do it. Temptation is the pull of my own evil thoughts and wishes. These evil thoughts lead to evil actions and afterwards to the death penalty from you. So I won't be misled.
James 1:13–16

Lead me not into temptation, and deliver me from the evil one.
Matthew 6:13

The Benefit of Resisting Temptation—III
No Temptation Is Irresistible

She kept putting pressure on him day after day, but he refused to sleep with her, and he kept out of her way as much as possible. One day, however, no one else was around when he was doing his work inside the house. She came and grabbed him by his shirt, demanding, "sleep with me!"
Joseph tore himself away, but as he did, his shirt came off. She was left holding it as he ran from the house.
—Genesis 39:10–12 NLT

Joseph's temptation was common. There is no such thing as a new temptation, too strong of a temptation, or a temptation that is irresistible. God always provides a way out.

The "Resisting Temptation" Challenge
- Do you believe God always provides a way to escape temptation?
- Do you see the benefit in simply running from temptation?
- Prepare yourself to resist temptation.

The "Resisting Temptation" Declarations

Father, I will remember this—the wrong desires that come into my life aren't anything new and different. Many others have faced exactly the same problems before me. And no temptation is irresistible. I can trust you to keep the temptation from becoming so strong that I can't stand up against it, for you have promised this and will do what you say. You will show me how to escape temptation's power so that I can bear up patiently against it.
1 Corinthians 10:13

This High Priest of mine understands my weaknesses since he had the same temptations I have, though he never once gave way to them and sinned. So I can come boldly to your very throne and stay there to receive your mercy and to find grace to help me in my times of need.
Hebrews 4:15–16

The Benefit of Rest—I
God Rested

"Remember the Sabbath day by keeping it holy. Six days you shall labor and do all your work, but the seventh day is a Sabbath to the Lord your God. On it you shall not do any work, neither you, nor your son or daughter, nor your manservant or maidservant, nor your animals, nor the alien within your gates.

For in six days the Lord made the heavens and the earth, the sea, and all that is in them, but he rested on the seventh day. Therefore the Lord blessed the Sabbath day and made it holy."

—Exodus 20:8–11 NIV

Rest is important to God—He invented it. In fact, rest is so important to God that He commands us to do it. It isn't just a suggestion. God created the Sabbath to serve us and refresh us. But it is not only the ceasing of work that brings us rest on this day, it is setting the day aside for the Lord.

God knows how human beings function best because He created us. Set aside this day for Him, and be refreshed.

The "Rest" Challenge

▸ Why is it important for you to honor the Sabbath?
▸ Is it possible for you to get your work done in six days?
▸▸ Meditate on how the Sabbath benefits you.

The "Rest" Declarations

Father, as I stand at the crossroads and look, I will ask for the ancient paths, I will ask where the good way is, and walk in it, and I will find rest for my soul.

Jeremiah 6:16

As I dwell in the shelter of the Most High, I will rest in the shadow of the Almighty.

Psalm 91:1

The Benefit of Rest—II
Jesus Rested

Very early in the morning, while it was still dark, Jesus got up, left the house and went off to a solitary place, where he prayed. Simon and his companions went to look for him, and when they found him, they exclaimed: "Everyone is looking for you!"
—Mark 1:35–37 NIV

People followed Jesus 24/7. He was always in high demand. Needy people continually pressed in on Him, expecting Him to do something for them. And yet, Jesus knew that the most important way to spend His time was with His Father.

We all understand too many needs surrounding us and too many demands on our time. If Jesus needed quiet time, how much more do we need it? When you take time to be in God's presence and to read His Word and pray, you'll find everything you need to get through the day.

The "Rest" Challenge

- Do you spend time alone with God each day?
- Are there too many demands on your time to have a quiet time?
- Think of a time when being with God refreshed you.

The "Rest" Declarations

Father, I will come to you when I am weary and burdened, and you will give me rest. I will take your yoke upon me and learn from you, for you are gentle and humble in heart, and I will find rest for my soul. For your yoke is easy and your burden is light.
Matthew 11:28–30

My soul finds rest in you alone.
Psalm 62:1

The Benefit of Rest—III
Mary Rested

As Jesus and his disciples were on their way, he came to a village where a woman named Martha opened her home to him. She had a sister called Mary, who sat at the Lord's feet listening to what he said.

But Martha was distracted by all the preparations that had to be made. She came to him and asked, "Lord, don't you care that my sister has left me to do the work by myself? Tell her to help me!"

"Martha, Martha," the Lord answered, "you are worried and upset about many things, but only one thing is needed. Mary has chosen what is better, and it will not be taken away from her."

—Luke 10:38–42 NIV

Martha was all worked up while Mary was resting at Jesus' feet. What a contrast! They both loved Jesus and wanted to serve Him, but each had very different ideas about how to do that.

Every day we have to choose whether to spend time doing one good thing or the other. Jesus said that Mary chose the only thing that was needed—she chose the best thing. Don't be so busy trying to serve Jesus that you forget to spend time at His feet.

The "Rest" Challenge

- Do you spend too much time serving Jesus, and not enough time being with Him?
- How can activities distract you from a relationship with God?
- Schedule time every day to sit at Jesus' feet.

The "Rest" Declarations

Father, you let me rest in the meadow grass and lead me beside the quiet streams.

Psalm 23:2

I will cease striving and know that you are God.

Psalm 46:10

The Benefit of Restoration—I
A Hand Restored

King Jeroboam was very angry with the man of God for speaking against the altar. So he pointed at the man and shouted, "Seize that man!" But instantly the king's hand became paralyzed in that position, and he couldn't pull it back. At the same time a wide crack appeared in the altar, and the ashes poured out, just as the man of God had predicted in his message from the Lord.

The king cried out to the man of God, "Please ask the Lord your God to restore my hand again!" So the man of God prayed to the Lord, and the kings' hand became normal again.
—1 Kings 13:4–6 NLT

A man of God from Judah went to Bethel right when King Jeroboam was offering a sacrifice. But King Jeroboam was not a Levite priest, Bethel was the wrong place to worship, and he was worshipping the wrong god. Jeroboam blatantly disregarded God's commands, so God was just in His judgment against him.

But when Jeroboam cried for mercy, God restored his hand. God wants to lovingly restore us—even when we mess up.

The "Restoration" Challenge

- Do you think God has ever been unjust to you?
- Are you waiting on God to restore you somehow?
- ▶▶ Reflect on a time when God restored you in some way.

The "Restoration" Declarations

Father, do not rebuke me in your anger or discipline me in your rage. Have compassion on me, Lord, for I am weak; heal me, Lord, for my body is in agony. I am sick at heart. How long, O Lord, until you restore me?

Psalm 6:1–3

Restore to me again the joy of your salvation, and make me willing to obey you.

Psalm 51:12 TLB

The Benefit of Restoration—II
A Life Restored

Then, when Job prayed for his friends, the Lord restored his wealth and happiness! In fact, the Lord gave him twice as much as before!
Then all of his brothers, sisters, and former friends arrived and feasted with him in his home, consoling him for all his sorrow, and comforting him because of all the trials the Lord had brought upon him. And each of them brought him a gift of money, and a gold ring.
So the Lord blessed Job at the end of his life more than at the beginning. For now he had 14,000 sheep, 6,000 camels, 1,000 teams of oxen, and 1,000 female donkeys.
God also gave him seven more sons and three more daughters.
—Job 42:10–13 TLB

Job, an upright man, was devoted to God and hated evil. One day, Satan devised a plan to divide Job and God through the loss of Job's children, his wealth, and his health. Job did nothing to deserve this.

Yet, Job never gave up on God, and God restored Job's life. In fact, God gave him twice as much as before.

The "Restoration" Challenge

- Do you believe God is able to restore that which is wrongly taken?
- Have you ever had anything taken from you unjustly?
- Consider if a personal loss has strained your relationship with God.

The "Restoration" Declarations

Father, restore our fortunes, like streams in the Negev. Those who sow in tears will reap with songs of joy. He who goes out weeping, carrying seed to sow, will return with songs of joy, carrying sheaves with him.
Psalm 126:4–6

You restore my soul.
Psalm 23:3

The Benefit of Restoration—III
A Home Restored

So the woman took her family and lived in the land of the Philistines for seven years. After the famine ended, she returned to the land of Israel and went to see the king about getting back her house and land. Just as she came in, the king was talking with Gehazi, Elisha's servant, and saying, "Tell me some stories of the great things Elisha has done." And Gehazi was telling the king about the time when Elisha brought a little boy back to life. At that very moment, the mother of the boy walked in!

"Oh, sir!" Gehazi exclaimed. "Here is the woman now, and this is her son—the very one Elisha brought back to life!"

"Is this true?" the king asked her. And she told him that it was. So he directed one of his officials to see to it that everything she had owned was restored to her, plus the value of any crops that had been harvested during her absence.

—2 Kings 8:2–6 TLB

Due to a famine, this woman had to move. Through circumstances beyond her control, she had to leave everything she owned behind. Now her family was returning home. Even though she was gone for so long, everything she owned was restored to her—plus more!

The "Restoration" Challenge

▸ Have you ever suffered a great loss that was beyond your control?
▸ Is there anything that is too difficult for God to restore?
▸▸ Meditate on God as your Restorer.

The "Restoration" Declarations

Father, you rebuild all of the ancient ruins in my life and restore the places long devastated.

Isaiah 61:4

Restore me, O God; make your face shine upon me, that I may be saved.

Psalm 80:3

The Benefit of Satisfaction—I
Living Water

A woman, a Samaritan, came to draw water. Jesus said, "Would you give me a drink of water?" (His disciples had gone to the village to buy food for lunch.)

The Samaritan woman, taken aback, asked, "How come you, a Jew, are asking me, a Samaritan woman, for a drink?" (Jews in those days wouldn't be caught dead talking to Samaritans.)

Jesus answered, "If you knew the generosity of God and who I am, you would be asking me for a drink, and I would give you fresh, living water."

—John 4:7–10

This woman was a Samaritan, which meant she was of a mixed race, part Jew and part foreigner. Also, she had a bad reputation because she had five husbands and was living with another man. To top it off, she was a woman. This Samaritan woman had three big strikes against her. Yet, Jesus cared enough to reach out to her.

Jesus knows that no matter where we've come from or what we've done, we need Him. We all have a spiritual thirst deep inside that only Jesus can satisfy.

The "Satisfaction" Challenge

- How do you feel knowing Jesus offers living water to everyone?
- Do you continually thirst for more of Jesus?
- Ask Jesus for a drink of His fresh, living water.

The "Satisfaction" Declarations

Father, as the deer pants for water, so I long for you.
Psalm 42:1

In you my soul will be satisfied as with the richest of foods.
Psalm 63:5

The Benefit of Satisfaction—II
Satisfaction Guaranteed

The woman said, "Sir, you don't even have a bucket to draw with, and this well is deep. So how are you going to get this 'living water'? Are you a better man than our ancestor Jacob, who dug this well and drank from it, he and his sons and livestock, and passed it down to us?"

—John 4:11–12

This Samaritan woman knew *about* God, and she knew a Messiah was to come. But she had yet to experience His life-giving water. Jesus knew that she had been disappointed by life and felt empty inside. He also knew just what was needed to fill her.

Even after we come to Christ and experience His life-giving water, we often look for satisfaction elsewhere. We try to fill our lives with pleasure, success, money, or relationships.

None of these things can ever take the place of God in our lives. If we continue to pursue them instead of God, we'll find ourselves empty and unsatisfied. But with God, our satisfaction is guaranteed.

The "Satisfaction" Challenge

▸ Where do you focus most of your attention and affection?
▸ Are you running on empty, needing a fill-up of living water?
▸▸ Confess to God if anything or anyone has taken His place in your life.

The "Satisfaction" Declarations

Father, whom have I in heaven but you? And earth has nothing I desire besides you.
My flesh and my heart may fail, but You are the strength of my heart and my portion forever.

Psalm 73:25–26

I will not forsake you, the Fountain of Life-giving Water; and I won't build for myself broken cisterns that can't hold water!

Jeremiah 2:13

The Benefit of Satisfaction—III
Give Me This Water

Jesus said, "Everyone who drinks this water will get thirsty again and again. Anyone who drinks the water I give will never thirst—not ever. The water I give will be an artesian spring within, gushing fountains of endless life."
The woman said, "Sir, give me this water so I won't ever get thirsty, won't ever have to come back to this well again!"
—John 4:13–15

Jesus told this woman that she needed only to ask to receive life-giving water—so she did. She was so excited about Jesus that she ran back to town and told everyone about Him. Because of her excitement and her testimony, many Samaritans from that town believed in Him.

When we experience the fountain of life that Jesus gives, we want to testify to those around us. We want others to experience what we've experienced. Help people to be aware of their need for Jesus, then, offer them His life-giving water.

The "Satisfaction" Challenge

- Do you tell others about the things Jesus does in your life?
- Have you had the joy of leading others to this life-giving water?
- Equip yourself to lead others to know Jesus as Savior.

The "Satisfaction" Declarations

Father, as I delight myself in you, you will give me the desires of my heart.
Psalm 37:4

You open your hand and satisfy all of my desires.
Psalm 145:16

The Benefit of Security—I
A Cork in the Storm

When a gentle southerly breeze came up, they weighed anchor, thinking it would be smooth sailing. But they were no sooner out to sea than a gale-force wind, the infamous nor'easter, struck. They lost all control of the ship. It was a cork in the storm.

We came under the lee of the small island named Clauda, and managed to get a lifeboat ready and reef the sails. But rocky shoals prevented us from getting close. We only managed to avoid them by throwing out drift anchors.

Next day, out on the high seas again and badly damaged now by the storm, we dumped the cargo overboard. The third day the sailors lightened the ship further by throwing off all the tackle and provisions. It had been many days since we had seen either sun or stars. Wind and waves were battering us unmercifully, and we lost all hope of rescue.

—Acts 27:13–20

Paul warned Julius (the centurion in charge), the pilot, and the owner of the ship that it was dangerous to set sail. But they decided to sail anyway, and ended up tossing around like a cork in the storm. So much for placing their security in man's sailing abilities or in the ship! Only God could make this voyage secure.

The "Security" Challenge

▸ Is there anything in life you can always depend on?
▸ What makes you feel safe?
▸▸ Memorize Proverbs 10:25.

The "Security" Declarations

Father, you hem me in—behind and before; you have laid your hand upon me.

Psalm 139:5

I have set you always before me. Because you are at my right hand, I will not be shaken.

Psalm 16:8

The Benefit of Security—II
We're Going to Make It

With our appetite for both food and life long gone, Paul took his place in our midst and said, "Friends, you really should have listened to me back in Crete. We could have avoided all this trouble and trial. But there's no need to dwell on that now. From now on, things are looking up! I can assure you that there'll not be a single drowning among us, although I can't say as much for the ship—the ship itself is doomed.

"Last night God's angel stood at my side, an angel of this God I serve, saying to me, 'Don't give up, Paul. You're going to stand before Caesar yet—and everyone sailing with you is also going to make it.' So, dear friends, take heart. I believe God will do exactly what he told me. But we're going to shipwreck on some island or other."
—Acts 27:21–26

God wanted Paul to stand trial before Caesar, so it was going to happen. Not only did God guarantee Paul's safe arrival, He also graciously spared the lives of everyone on the ship.

God gave Paul a firm place to stand, and He wants to do the same for you.

The "Security" Challenge

- Have you ever been disappointed after placing your security in things of this world?
- Is there something in your life now that causes you to feel unstable?
- Consider what you need to entrust into God's hands for safekeeping.

The "Security" Declarations

Father, I am convinced that you are able to guard all that I have entrusted to you.
2 Timothy 1:12

You set my feet on a rock and give me a firm place to stand.
Psalm 40:2

The Benefit of Security—III
Security in a Lifeboat?

On the fourteenth night, adrift somewhere on the Adriatic Sea, at about midnight the sailors sensed that we were approaching land. Sounding, they measured a depth of one hundred twenty feet, and shortly after that ninety feet. Afraid that we were about to run aground, they threw out four anchors and prayed for daylight.

Some of the sailors tried to jump ship. They let down the lifeboat, pretending they were going to set out more anchors from the bow. Paul saw through their guise and told the centurion and his soldiers, "If these sailors don't stay with the ship, we're all going down." So the soldiers cut the lines to the lifeboat and let it drift off.

With dawn about to break, Paul called everyone together and proposed breakfast: "This is the fourteenth day we've gone without food. None of us has felt like eating! But I urge you to eat something now. You'll need strength for the rescue ahead. You're going to come out of this without even a scratch!"

—Acts 27:27–34

Bank accounts, relationships, jobs, abilities, and Homeland Security can give us a false sense of security, like the lifeboats on this ship. God, however, is steady and unchanging—He is your rock. He isn't affected by the economy or by downsizing or by wars or by the storms of life that rock your boat.

The "Security" Challenge

▸ Can you find security in anyone or anything other than God?
▸ What would be the benefit of having God as your sole source of security?
▸▸ Identify the "lifeboats" in your life, and then turn to God for security.

The "Security" Declarations

Father, you have made my lot secure.

Psalm 16:5

Because of you, my heart is steady.

Psalm 112:8

The Benefit of Self-Control—I
Food and Wine from the King's Table

In the third year of the reign of Jehoiakim king of Judah, Nebuchadnezzar king of Babylon came to Jerusalem and besieged it. And the Lord delivered Jehoiakim king of Judah into his hand, along with some of the articles from the temple of God. These he carried off to the temple of his god in Babylonia and put in the treasure house of his god.

Then the king ordered Ashpenaz, chief of his court officials, to bring in some of the Israelites from the royal family and the nobility—young men without any physical defect, handsome, showing aptitude for every kind of learning, well informed, quick to understand, and qualified to serve in the king's palace.

He was to teach them the language and literature of the Babylonians. The king assigned them a daily amount of food and wine from the king's table. They were to be trained for three years, and after that they were to enter the king's service.

—Daniel 1:1–5 NIV

Daniel was taken captive into a strange land where God was not worshipped. Now that Daniel was far from home, he had the opportunity to indulge in a whole new lifestyle. After all, the king expected it.

The "Self-Control" Challenge

▸ When do you find it hard to maintain self-control?
▸ Do you show self-control only when you're around other Christians?
▸▸ Ask God to help you with any self-control issues.

The "Self-Control" Declarations

Father, I won't drink too much wine, for many evils lie along that path; but I will be filled instead with the Holy Spirit and controlled by him.

Ephesians 5:18

It's better for me to have self-control than for me to control an entire army.

Proverbs 16:32

The Benefit of Self-Control—II
Daniel's Resolve

But Daniel resolved not to defile himself with the royal food and wine, and he asked the chief official for permission not to defile himself this way. Now God had caused the official to show favor and sympathy to Daniel, but the official told Daniel, "I am afraid of my lord the king, who has assigned your food and drink. Why should he see you looking worse than the other young men your age? The king would then have my head because of you."

Daniel then said to the guard whom the chief official had appointed over Daniel, Hananiah, Mishael and Azariah, "Please test your servants for ten days: Give us nothing but vegetables to eat and water to drink. Then compare our appearance with that of the young men who eat the royal food, and treat your servants in accordance with what you see." So he agreed to this and tested them for ten days.
—Daniel 1:8–14 NIV

These menu choices didn't appear to be difficult for Daniel. He was committed to God and His ways, and he lived his life accordingly. Self-control is the resolve to consistently say *no* to worldly passions and *yes* to God's Spirit.

The "Self-Control" Challenge

▸ Are you more controlled by physical appetites or by spiritual ones?
▸ How can you make self-control a consistent way of life?
▶ Practice saying no to worldly passions and yes to God's Spirit.

The "Self-Control" Declarations

Father, it is your grace that brought salvation to me and that teaches me to say "No" to ungodliness and worldly passions, and to live a self-controlled, upright and godly life.
Titus 2:11–12

I am controlled by my new nature because I have your Spirit living in me.
Romans 8:9

The Benefit of Self-Control—III
No Equal

At the end of the ten days they looked healthier and better nourished than any of the young men who ate the royal food. So the guard took away their choice food and the wine they were to drink and gave them vegetables instead.

To these four young men God gave knowledge and understanding of all kinds of literature and learning. And Daniel could understand visions and dreams of all kinds.

At the end of the time set by the king to bring them in, the chief official presented them to Nebuchadnezzar. The king talked with them, and he found none equal to Daniel, Hananiah, Mishael and Azariah; so they entered the king's service. In every matter of wisdom and understanding about which the king questioned them, he found them ten times better than all the magicians and enchanters in his whole kingdom.

—Daniel 1:15–20 NIV

Compare what Daniel gained from self-control to what the lack of it caused others to lose. Eve lost paradise, Cain lost a brother, Esau lost a birthright, and Samson lost his strength. Self-control gives life, and self-indulgence takes it away.

The "Self-Control" Challenge

- Have you experienced the fruit of self-control in your life?
- What does self-indulgence gain you?
- Ask God's Spirit daily to control your life.

The "Self-Control" Declarations

Father, it is your will that I should be sanctified: that I should avoid sexual immorality; that I should learn to control my own body in a way that is holy and honorable, not in passionate lust like the heathen, who do not know you.

1 Thessalonians 4:3–6

When I allow your Holy Spirit to control my life, you will produce the fruit of self-control in me.

Galatians 5:22–23

The Benefit of Success—I
The Lord Will Make Your Mission Successful

"Now when Sarah, my master's wife, was very old, she gave birth to my master's son, and my master has given him everything he owns. And my master made me promise not to let Isaac marry one of the local girls, but to come to his relatives here in this far-off land, to his brother's family, and to bring back a girl from here to marry his son. 'But suppose I can't find a girl who will come?' I asked him. 'She will,' he told me—'for my Lord, in whose presence I have walked, will send his angel with you and make your mission successful. Yes, find a girl from among my relatives, from my brother's family. You are under oath to go and ask. If they won't send anyone, then you are freed from your promise.'"

—Genesis 24:36–41 TLB

Abraham sent his servant to a far-off land to find a wife for his son, Isaac. God wanted this to happen. So, Abraham sent his servant with the assurance that the Lord would help him achieve his goal. What a great way to start a mission!

The "Success" Challenge

▸ Has God ever given you the assurance that you will succeed?
▸ What in the past has caused your plans to fail?
▸▸ Commit your plans to the Lord and they will succeed.

The "Success" Declarations

Father, if my purpose or activity is of human origin, it will fail. But if it is from you, it will not be able to be stopped.
Acts 5:38–39

As I commit to you whatever I do, my plans will succeed.
Proverbs 16:3

The Benefit of Success—II
The Servant Asked for a Sign

"Well, this afternoon when I came to the spring I prayed this prayer: 'O Jehovah, the God of my master Abraham, if you are planning to make my mission a success, please guide me in this way: Here I am, standing beside this spring. I will say to some girl who comes out to draw water, "Please give me a drink of water!" And she will reply, "Certainly! And I'll water your camels too!" Let that girl be the one you have selected to be the wife of my master's son.'"
—Genesis 24:42–44 TLB

When Abraham's servant arrived in the city of Nahor, he continued to make God part of his plans by praying. It's great to commit new plans to the Lord. It's also important to keep God as the CEO of the process while you move forward. God is the One responsible for your successes, and He ensures you achieve results that are important to Him.

God has no interest in futile or self-serving plans that bring you riches or power or prestige. He wants to help you achieve success that results in eternal rewards.

The "Success" Challenge

- Do you align your plans with God's, or try to make God fit in with your plans?
- Are you reaching for successes that are futile or self-serving?
- ▸ Seek God for specific steps you can take toward success.

The "Success" Declarations

Father, in everything I do, as I put you first, you will direct me and crown my efforts with success.
                                                    Proverbs 3:6

As I work hard, I will be successful.
                                                    Proverbs 22:29

The Benefit of Success—III
The Right Path

"Well, while I was still speaking these words, Rebekah was coming along with her water jug upon her shoulder; and she went down to the spring and drew water and filled the jug. I said to her, 'Please give me a drink.'

"She quickly lifted the jug down from her shoulder so that I could drink, and told me, 'Certainly, sir, and I will water your camels too!' So she did! Then I asked her, 'Whose family are you from?' And she told me, 'Nahor's. My father is Bethuel, the son of Nahor and his wife Milcah.'

"So I gave her the ring and the bracelets. Then I bowed my head and worshiped and blessed Jehovah, the God of my master Abraham, because he had led me along just the right path to find a girl from the family of my master's brother."
—Genesis 24:45–48 TLB

The servant barely got the prayer out when along came Rebekah. God led him along the right path to find the right girl—he achieved what he set out to do. His success was from God, the kind that feels good.

There are times in life when success leaves us feeling lonely or empty—that's not true success. Those kinds of achievements are meaningless.

God is the center of every true success, and He gets the glory.

The "Success" Challenge
- Has success ever left you feeling empty?
- Do you give God glory for your successes?
- Evaluate how you measure success.

The "Success" Declarations

Father, I cannot do anything of lasting value by myself. My only power and success comes from you.
2 Corinthians 3:4–5

As I obey your Word, I will succeed.
Proverbs 13:13

The Benefit of Thanksgiving—I
An Attitude of Gratitude

It happened that as [Jesus] made his way toward Jerusalem, he crossed over the border between Samaria and Galilee. As he entered a village, ten men, all lepers, met him. They kept their distance but raised their voices, calling out, "Jesus, Master, have mercy on us!"

Taking a good look at them, he said, "Go, show yourselves to the priests."

They went, and while still on their way, became clean. One of them, when he realized that he was healed, turned around and came back, shouting his gratitude, glorifying God. He kneeled at Jesus' feet, so grateful. He couldn't thank him enough—and he was a Samaritan.

Jesus said, "Were not ten healed? Where are the nine? Can none be found to come back and give glory to God except this outsider?" Then he said to him, "Get up. On your way. Your faith has healed and saved you."

—Luke 17:11–17

The ten lepers cried out to Jesus for healing. Most of us do that part well—cry out to God. But some of us fail to offer thanksgiving to Him.

More often, we should simply thank Him for who He is and for everything that He's done.

The "Thanksgiving" Challenge

▸ Do you have an attitude of gratitude toward God?
▸ How important to God is a grateful heart?
▸▸ Make thanksgiving part of every prayer you pray.

The "Thanksgiving" Declarations

Father, it is good for me to say thank you for your kindness in the morning, and rejoice in your faithfulness at night.
Psalm 92:1–2

I constantly boast about you. I can never thank you enough!
Psalm 44:8–9

The Benefit of Thanksgiving—II
Give Thanks to the Lord

Give thanks to the Lord, for he is good!
His faithful love endures forever.
Give thanks to the God of gods.
His faithful love endures forever.
Give thanks to the Lord of lords.
His faithful love endures forever.
Give thanks to him who alone does mighty miracles.
His faithful love endures forever.
Give thanks to him who made the heavens so skillfully.
His faithful love endures forever.
Give thanks to him who placed the earth on the water.
His faithful love endures forever.
—Psalm 136:1–6 NLT

There is no end to the things we can thank God for. Just begin by thanking Him for His wonderful creation, His mercy and goodness, His unconditional love, His faithfulness, and many other things will come to mind.

When you offer thanksgiving to God, your heart can change from a grumbling heart to an uplifted one.

The "Thanksgiving" Challenge

- Do you remember to thank God for answered prayers?
- Have you noticed how uplifting a thankful heart can be?
- Thank God right now for the work of His hands.

The "Thanksgiving" Declarations

Father, I will go through your open gates with great thanksgiving; and enter your courts with praise. I give thanks to you and bless your name.
Psalm 100:4–5

Oh, how grateful and thankful I am to you because you are so good. I will sing praise to the name of the Lord who is above all lords.
Psalm 7:17

The Benefit of Thanksgiving—III
In Everything Give Thanks

Give thanks to him who led his people through the wilderness.
His faithful love endures forever.
He remembered our utter weakness.
His faithful love endures forever.
He saved us from our enemies.
His faithful love endures forever.
He gives food to every living thing.
His faithful love endures forever.
Give thanks to the God of heaven.
His faithful love endures forever.
—Psalm 136:16, 23–26 NLT

Sometimes difficult circumstances make it hard to have a grateful heart. But it is God's will for us to give thanks in *all* circumstances. No matter where we are in life, we can thank Him for saving us and giving us life, and for taking such great care of us.

We can even thank Him for the good that is to come. So walk in His will for you today and offer thanks to Him—it will literally give you a new outlook.

The "Thanksgiving" Challenge

▸ What are you grateful for today?
▸ When is it hard for you to be thankful?
▸▸ Ask God to foster in you a thankful heart in all circumstances.

The "Thanksgiving" Declarations

Father, no matter what happens, I will always be thankful, for this is your will for me.
1 Thessalonians 5:18

O Lord, thank you so much for answering my prayer and saving me.
Psalm 118:21 TLB

The Benefit of Trust—I
A Little Boat—A Lot of Trust

There were at this time a Hebrew fellow and girl of the tribe of Levi who married and had a family, and a baby son was born to them. When the baby's mother saw that he was an unusually beautiful baby, she hid him at home for three months.

Then, when she could no longer hide him, she made a little boat from papyrus reeds, waterproofed it with tar, put the baby in it, and laid it among the reeds along the river's edge. The baby's sister watched from a distance to see what would happen to him.
—Exodus 2:1–4 TLB

Pharaoh ordered all Hebrew baby boys to be killed. So, this baby boy was going into the Nile one way or another—either by an act of evil or by an act of trust. His mother chose to trust God.

God is worthy of our trust because He is completely reliable. He is not fickle, He does not change, and He is not deceitful. God sees the big picture and works things out for the greatest good. Even when we don't understand what God is up to, we can put our confidence in Him.

The "Trust" Challenge

▸ Do you always believe that God is worthy of your trust?
▸ Has your confidence in God ever been shaken?
▸▸ In an act of trust, give your hard-to-understand situation to God.

The "Trust" Declarations

Father, I will trust in you with all my heart and lean not on my own understanding; in all my ways I will acknowledge you, and you will make my paths straight.
Proverbs 3:5–6

I am trusting you, you alone are my God; my times are in your hands.
Psalm 31:14

The Benefit of Trust—II
Don't Put Your Confidence in People

Well, this is what happened: A princess, one of Pharaoh's daughters, came down to bathe in the river, and as she and her maids were walking along the river bank, she spied the little boat among the reeds and sent one of the maids to bring it to her.

When she opened it, there was a baby! And he was crying. This touched her heart. "He must be one of the Hebrew children!" she said.

—Exodus 2:5–6 TLB

God was busy working out all the details. He arranged for this Egyptian princess to see the baby during her bath time. The little baby touched her heart and she wanted to keep him. All of this happened because of a mother's heart that trusted in God.

God says that it benefits us when we put our confidence in Him rather than in people. People will fail us. They're just not capable of being completely dependable, as God is. People change, are wishy-washy, aren't always pure in their motives, aren't always truthful, and won't always be there for you. God will!

The "Trust" Challenge

- Have you ever trusted in someone who failed you?
- Do you tend to put your confidence in God or in people?
- Consider the difference between trusting in God and trusting in people.

The "Trust" Declarations

Father, as I trust in you and put my confidence in you, I will be blessed. I will be like a tree planted by the water that sends out its roots by the stream.

Jeremiah 17:7–8

It is better for me to trust you than to put my confidence in people.

Psalm 118:8

The Benefit of Trust—III
To Know God Is to Trust God

Then the baby's sister approached the princess and asked her, "Shall I go and find one of the Hebrew women to nurse the baby for you?"

"Yes, do!" the princess replied. So the little girl rushed home and called her mother!

"Take this child home and nurse him for me," the princess instructed the baby's mother, "and I will pay you well!" So she took him home and nursed him.

Later, when he was older, she brought him back to the princess and he became her son. She named him Moses (meaning "to draw out") because she had drawn him out of the water.
—Exodus 2:7–10 TLB

The baby's sister approached the princess with a bold request, taking advantage of a divine opportunity. Because she did, Moses was saved, his own mother got to nurse him, and she was paid to do it.

When we face challenges, we discover where we put our trust. The more we get to know God, the more we develop an assurance that God really can be trusted with everything—eternity, marriage, children, the future, a job, health, challenges, a home, our very lives.

The "Trust" Challenge

- Do you sometimes put more confidence in yourself than you do in God?
- How can challenges show us where we put our trust?
- Make getting to know God your priority.

The "Trust" Declarations

Father, I will not fear bad news, nor live in dread of what may happen. For it is settled in my mind that you will take care of me.
Psalm 112:6–8

You have never yet forsaken those who trust in you.
Psalm 9:10

The Benefit of Victory in Battle—I
The Right Mindset for Battle

Then Saul gave David his own armor—a bronze helmet and a coat of mail. David put it on, strapped the sword over it, and took a step or two to see what it was like, for he had never worn such things before.

"I can't go in these," he protested. "I'm not used to them." So he took them off again. He picked up five smooth stones from a stream and put them in his shepherd's bag. Then, armed only with his shepherd's staff and sling, he started across to fight Goliath.
—1 Samuel 17:38–40 NLT

Young David hadn't yet gone through boot camp. But he did have experience in submitting to God and in resisting enemies. As a shepherd, he bravely fought off anything that tried to harm his flock.

David was willing to do the same with this giant, Goliath, who dared to defy the armies of the living God. David had the right mindset for battle. He knew that the same God who gave him victory over lions and bears would give him victory over the giant.

Every Israelite soldier believed the battle was impossible to win. David believed it was impossible to lose. Be victory minded!

The "Victory in Battle" Challenge

- Are you in the habit of submitting to God and resisting the enemy?
- How is your mind a battleground?
- Cultivate a mindset like David's in the battles you face.

The "Victory in Battle" Declarations

Father, not by my might nor by my power, but by your Spirit will I have victory.
Zechariah 4:6

Lord, with you on my side, who can ever be against me?
Romans 8:31

The Benefit of Victory in Battle—II
The Battle Belongs to the Lord

Goliath walked out toward David with his shield bearer ahead of him, sneering in contempt at this ruddy-faced boy. "Am I a dog," he roared at David, "that you come at me with a stick?" And he cursed David by the names of his gods. "Come over here, and I'll give your flesh to the birds and wild animals!" Goliath yelled.

David shouted in reply, "You come to me with sword, spear, and javelin, but I come to you in the name of the Lord Almighty—the God of the armies of Israel, whom you have defied.

"Today the Lord will conquer you, and I will kill you and cut off your head. And then I will give the dead bodies of your men to the birds and wild animals, and the whole world will know that there is a God in Israel! And everyone will know that the Lord does not need weapons to rescue his people. It is his battle, not ours. The Lord will give you to us!"

—1 Samuel 17:41–47 NLT

David knew that man's finest-fashioned armor, weapons, and strategies could not give him victory over his enemy. The Lord would fight for him.

The "Victory in Battle" Challenge

- What are some of your battle strategies that have failed?
- Do you try to win your own battles?
- ▶ Stand strong with a friend who's fighting a battle.

The "Victory in Battle" Declarations

Father, I do not trust my weapons. They could never save me. Only you can give me the victory over my enemies.
Psalm 44:6–7

I thank you that I am more than a conqueror through you.
Romans 8:37

The Benefit of Victory in Battle—III
Victory Over My Enemy

As Goliath moved closer to attack, David quickly ran out to meet him. Reaching into his shepherd's bag and taking out a stone, he hurled it from his sling and hit the Philistine in the forehead. The stone sank in, and Goliath stumbled and fell face downward to the ground.
So David triumphed over the Philistine giant with only a stone and sling.
—1 Samuel 17:48–50 NLT

Goliath was just the first of many casualties in this battle. After the Philistines saw that their champion fighter was dead, they turned and ran. The Israelites then pursued them, triumphed over them, and took their treasure.

We, like David, are engaged in battle against an enemy who seeks to defy the living God—and anyone who follows Him. His name is Satan. He was once a formidable enemy that held us captive. But Jesus triumphed over him through the cross, and we no longer need to fear him.

Satan still prowls around looking for ways to attack us, but he has been disarmed and rendered powerless against us. Let's remember whom our enemy is and that our weapons are mighty. We will stand our ground and overcome with God's Spirit, God's Word, and prayer.

The "Victory in Battle" Challenge

- What are some ways that Satan attacks you?
- Are you ever confused as to whom the real enemy is?
- Thank God that Jesus has already triumphed over your enemies.

The "Victory in Battle" Declarations

Father, I will use your mighty weapons, not those made by men, to knock down the devil's strongholds.
2 Corinthians 10:4

I thank you that no weapon formed against me will prosper.
Isaiah 54:17

The Benefit of Waiting on God—I
God's Timing Is Impeccable

We were slaves to Jewish laws and rituals for we thought they could save us. But when the right time came, the time God decided on, he sent his Son, born of a woman, born as a Jew, to buy freedom for us who were slaves to the law so that he could adopt us as his very own sons.
— Galatians 4:3b–5 TLB

God sent His Son, Jesus, when the fullness of time came. It was the perfect time for the prophecies concerning the Messiah to be fulfilled. Because God knew when the world would be spiritually ripe. He also knew the best time politically, socially, and morally.

Just as Jesus came into the world at the most beneficial time, He also started His ministry at just the right time. Jesus came to save the world, yet He patiently worked as a carpenter in Nazareth until He was thirty. That's a long time to wait to start a *Save the World Ministry*!

Just like Jesus, we need to wait for God's impeccable timing.

The "Waiting on God" Challenge

- Has God placed something on your heart that you're impatient to see Him fulfill?
- When do you have the urge to jump ahead of God's timing?
- With 20/20 vision, look back to see God's perfect timing in your life.

The "Waiting on God" Declarations

Father, you are not slow in keeping your promise, as some understand slowness. You are patient with us, not wanting anyone to perish, but everyone to come to repentance.
2 Peter 3:9

There's an opportune time to do things, a right time for everything on earth.
Ecclesiastes 3:1

The Benefit of Waiting on God—II
If Only You Had Been Here

On his arrival, Jesus found that Lazarus had already been in the tomb for four days. Bethany was less than two miles from Jerusalem, and many Jews had come to Martha and Mary to comfort them in the loss of their brother. When Martha heard that Jesus was coming, she went out to meet him, but Mary stayed at home.

"Lord," Martha said to Jesus, "if you had been here, my brother would not have died. But I know that even now God will give you whatever you ask."

— John 11:17–22 NIV

Word came to Jesus from Mary and Martha that their brother Lazarus was very sick. Jesus knew this was an occasion to show God's glory, yet He and His followers stayed away for two more days.

Then Jesus knew it was time to go to Lazarus. When they arrived, Lazarus had been in the tomb for four days. From Martha's perspective, Jesus was slow to come and could have saved her brother if He had come sooner.

God is never fashionably late—He does everything with incredible purpose.

The "Waiting on God" Challenge

- Does it ever seem that God is slow to take action?
- Why does it benefit you to wait for God's timing?
- Tell God you trust His timing enough to wait.

The "Waiting on God" Declarations

Father, if I must keep trusting you for something that hasn't happened yet, it teaches me to wait patiently and confidently.

Romans 8:25

I will wait patiently for you to act.

Psalm 37:7

The Benefit of Waiting on God—III
So That They Might Believe

So they took away the stone. Then Jesus looked up and said, "Father, I thank you that you have heard me. I knew that you always hear me, but I said this for the benefit of the people standing here, that they may believe that you sent me."

When he had said this, Jesus called in a loud voice, "Lazarus, come out!" The dead man came out, his hands and feet wrapped with strips of linen, and a cloth around his face.

Jesus said to them, "Take off the grave clothes and let him go."

Therefore many of the Jews who had come to visit Mary, and had seen what Jesus did, put their faith in him.
—John 11:41–45 NIV

Every detail was divinely deliberate and well timed.

First, many people gathered to mourn the death of Lazarus. So, Jesus knew many would witness His resurrection power, and understand that He was the Son of God.

Second, all of Israel had gathered in Jerusalem at this time for the annual Passover celebration. The crowds were about to witness the perfect Passover Lamb.

When we wait on God's timing, we can count on maximum impact.

The "Waiting on God" Challenge

- What has your impatience caused you to miss?
- Do you see that waiting on God has potential for greater impact?
- Remind a friend that God's timing is worth the wait.

The "Waiting on God" Declarations

Father, I won't be impatient for you to act! I will keep traveling steadily along your pathway and in due season you will honor me with every blessing.
Psalm 37:34

The moment I get tired in the waiting, your Spirit is right alongside helping me along.
Romans 8:26

The Benefit of Wisdom—I
No Wisdom Apart from God

Happy is the person who finds wisdom and gains understanding. For the profit of wisdom is better than silver, and her wages are better than gold. Wisdom is more precious than rubies; nothing you desire can compare with her. She offers you life in her right hand, and riches and honor in her left.

She will guide you down delightful paths; all her ways are satisfying. Wisdom is a tree of life to those who embrace her; happy are those who hold her tightly.

By wisdom the Lord founded the earth; by understanding he established the heavens. By his knowledge the deep fountains of the earth burst forth, and the clouds poured down rain.
—Proverbs 3:13–20 NLT

How do we find wisdom? We don't need to have a college degree or be a philosopher, a genius, or even a pastor to find it. In fact, we can't even begin to find wisdom apart from God, no matter who we are.

We find wisdom when we reverence God, when we cease to be impressed with what we know, and when we realize that in comparison to God's wisdom, ours is "fool's gold"—it amounts to nothing.

Godly wisdom is not fashionable, volatile, or contemporary; it is solid and stands the test of time—it is a true gold mine.

The "Wisdom" Challenge

- Do you believe you can find wisdom apart from God?
- How have you profited from wisdom in your life?
- Consider the value of godly wisdom.

The "Wisdom" Declarations

Father, how can I be wise? The only way to begin is by reverencing you. I will grow in wisdom as I obey your laws.
Psalm 111:10

Lord, you are wonderful in counsel and magnificent in wisdom.
Isaiah 28:29

The Benefit of Wisdom—II
Everyday Wisdom

The next day Moses took his seat to serve as judge for the people, and they stood around him from morning till evening. When his father-in-law saw all that Moses was doing for the people, he said, "What is this you are doing for the people? Why do you alone sit as judge, while all these people stand around you from morning till evening?"

Moses answered him, "Because the people come to me to seek God's will. Whenever they have a dispute, it is brought to me, and I decide between the parties and inform them of God's decrees and laws."

Moses' father-in-law replied, "What you are doing is not good. You and these people who come to you will only wear yourselves out. The work is too heavy for you; you cannot handle it alone."
—Exodus 18:13–18 NIV

Wisdom is the ability to apply God-given knowledge to everyday life. Moses' father-in-law stepped in to prevent Moses from burning out. He knew that Moses was trying to handle too much on his own and that there was a better way.

God desires to offer wisdom in everyday practical matters. We need only ask.

The "Wisdom" Challenge

- In what situation do you need wisdom from God?
- Has God ever given you knowledge you chose not to apply?
- Make it your habit to ask God for wisdom in practical matters.

The "Wisdom" Declarations

Father, if I want to know what you want me to do, I will ask you, and you will gladly tell me, for you are always ready to give a bountiful supply of wisdom to all who ask you.
James 1:5

You teach me wisdom in the inmost place.
Psalm 51:6b NIV

The Benefit of Wisdom—III
The Wisdom Test

"Listen now to me and I will give you some advice, and may God be with you. You must be the people's representative before God and bring their disputes to him. Teach them the decrees and laws, and show them the way to live and the duties they are to perform.

"But select capable men from all the people—men who fear God, trustworthy men who hate dishonest gain—and appoint them as officials over thousands, hundreds, fifties and tens. Have them serve as judges for the people at all times, but have them bring every difficult case to you; the simple cases they can decide themselves.

"That will make your load lighter, because they will share it with you. If you do this and God so commands, you will be able to stand the strain, and all these people will go home satisfied."

Moses listened to his father-in-law and did everything he said.

—Exodus 18:19–24 NIV

How do we know if someone is wise? By their actions. Godly wisdom shows itself in actions that are pure and sincere, gentle, considerate and merciful, impartial, and peace loving. Godly wisdom yields to others and produces good fruit.

The "Wisdom" Challenge

- Does your life produce good fruit?
- Do others turn to you for wisdom and understanding?
- Test your actions today to determine if they are wise or foolish.

The "Wisdom" Declarations

Father, the wisdom that comes from you is first of all pure; then peace-loving, considerate, submissive, full of mercy and good fruit, impartial and sincere.

James 3:17

You guide me in the way of wisdom and lead me along straight paths.

Proverbs 4:11

The Benefit of Worth—I
In His Image

Who has believed our message? To whom will the Lord reveal his saving power? My servant grew up in the Lord's presence like a tender green shoot, sprouting from a root in dry and sterile ground. There was nothing beautiful or majestic about his appearance, nothing to attract us to him.

He was despised and rejected—a man of sorrows, acquainted with bitterest grief. We turned our backs on him and looked the other way when he went by. He was despised, and we did not care.
—Isaiah 53:1–3 NLT

Jesus, who was the exact image of God in human form, left His glory and majesty behind so He could be like us, dwell among us, and reach out to us.

This Scripture says that nothing in Jesus' appearance would attract us to Him, and that the world despised and rejected Him. But Jesus didn't seek His worth from the world, He found it in His Father.

God created each of us in His image and we are wonderfully made. Because we are His creation, we dare not criticize ourselves or we would be criticizing the work of God's hands. Don't let the world determine your worth—let God!

The "Worth" Challenge

- In what ways are you critical of yourself?
- Do you measure your worth according to the world's standards, or God's?
- Tell someone that they are wonderfully created in God's image.

The "Worth" Declarations

Father, you created my inmost being; you knit me together in my mother's womb. I praise you because I am fearfully and wonderfully made; your works are wonderful, I know that full well.
Psalm 139:13–14

You created me in your own image.
Genesis 1:27

The Benefit of Worth—II
Jesus Thought You Were Worth Dying For

Yet it was our weaknesses he carried; it was our sorrows that weighed him down. And we thought his troubles were a punishment from God for his own sins! But he was wounded and crushed for our sins. He was beaten that we might have peace. He was whipped, and we were healed!

All of us have strayed away like sheep. We have left God's paths to follow our own. Yet the Lord laid on him the guilt and sins of us all.

He was oppressed and treated harshly, yet he never said a word. He was led as a lamb to the slaughter. And as a sheep is silent before the shearers, he did not open his mouth. From prison and trial they led him away to his death.

But who among the people realized that he was dying for their sins—that he was suffering their punishment? He had done no wrong, and he never deceived anyone.
—Isaiah 53:4–9 NLT

It has been said that the value of something is determined by the price someone is willing to pay for it. You are so precious to Jesus that He paid for your life by sacrificing His own. Jesus thought you were worth it.

The "Worth" Challenge

- How do you feel knowing that Jesus was crushed for your sins?
- Do you believe you are precious to Jesus?
- Thank God that Jesus considered you worth dying for.

The "Worth" Declarations

Father, because of what Christ has done, I am a gift to you and you delight in me;
I have been chosen from the beginning to be yours.
Ephesians 1:11

You have bought me with a great price.
1 Corinthians 6:20

The Benefit of Worth—III
I Have Called You Friends

My command is this: Love each other as I have loved you. Greater love has no one than this, that he lay down his life for his friends.

You are my friends if you do what I command. I no longer call you servants, because a servant does not know his master's business. Instead, I have called you friends, for everything that I learned from my Father I have made known to you.

You did not choose me, but I chose you and appointed you to go and bear fruit—fruit that will last.
—John 15:12–16 NIV

God does not want us to think more highly or lowly of ourselves than we ought to. Either way, it hurts Him and is harmful to us. He wants us to have a healthy, honest estimation of our worth and to see ourselves the way that He does.

He cares about how we see ourselves and how we see others. He wants us to value all people the way that He does. We have been equally created, esteemed, loved, and chosen. He calls us friends!

The "Worth" Challenge

- How do you feel knowing that God has called you His friend?
- Do you ever think more highly of yourself than you should?
- Ask God to help you see yourself the way He sees you.

The "Worth" Declarations

Father, I will not think of myself more highly than I ought, but will rather think of myself with sober judgment, in accordance with the measure of faith you have given me.
Romans 12:3

I am your workmanship, created in Christ Jesus to do good works, which you prepared in advance for me to do.
Ephesians 2:10

Printed in the United States
40439LVS00006B/103-159